What People Are Saying About

Heathenry for the Solitary Practitioner

With Thea's signature warm and engaging writing style, I felt welcomed into this introduction to modern Heathenry, which blends mythology and history with practical advice. Whether you're just starting out or already on your path, Thea offers thoughtful guidance to help you connect with ancient wisdom in a meaningful way. This is a great resource for anyone curious about exploring these traditions today.
Sarah Robinson, author of *Kitchen Witch: Food, Folklore & Fairy Tale, The Witch and the Wildwood,* and *Witch Country*

Heathenry for the Solitary Practitioner is a great addition to any Heathen's library. Written for those who are approaching Heathenry alone it covers all the basics from a fresh perspective. Perfect for the individual looking to learn about or begin practicing Norse spirituality.
Morgan Daimler, author of *Pantheon: The Norse* and *Pagan Portals: Freya, Odin & Thor*

This book is a comprehensive starter kit for exploring Heathen religion and connecting with the Norse and Anglo-Saxon deities. Written from a reassuringly inclusive perspective, it begins with the history, cosmology, and pantheon of Heathen spiritual practice. On this strong foundation, the author then unfolds a set of practices that are accessible and fulfilling for the solitary practitioner. Discover the rituals and sacred festivals that will add meaning to your year, and the divination methods that will provide insight into your life. This book is for everyone, everywhere with an interest in this powerful and fascinating spiritual tradition.
Laura Perry, author of *Pantheon: The Minoans*

A fascinating and informative read detailing Heathenry from its origin and what it represents today. Thea explores the similarities and differences between Vikings and Anglo-Saxons for balance on what was happening in England at the time. The Norse Edda's, poems to their gods, their deeds, wisdom and mythology and the Sagas of the Saxons including the epic *Beowulf* are expertly researched. *Heathenry for the Solitary Practitioner* includes some beautiful devotions to the Heathen deities and describes how to write your own heartfelt prayers to them and a very substantial and personal clarification interpretation of the runes. Significantly, the book includes an examination of Heathen women within the Viking and Anglo-Saxon culture and interviews of prominent Heathen women on their place within modern Heathen practice.
Scott Irvine, author of *The Magic of Serpents* and *Ishtar and Ereshkigal*

Heathen for the Solitary Practitioner gives a clear and practical introduction to the Northern European Tradition and its practices, allowing those interested in traveling this path a springboard from which they can develop their own relationship to those deities and beings through the rituals and celebrations, thoughtfully adapted for those who wish to follow a solitary path. Thea Prothero has been a solitary Heathen for many years and shows how using the *Völuspá, Hávamál,* and Eddas, readers can gain an understanding of how people of this era saw their world and interacted with the Gods and ancestors. Thea also gives an in-depth introduction to the Runes for anyone who wishes to study them. She highlights organizations for anyone who wishes to reach out to others within the community. A very useful guide for the beginner.
Martha Gray, author of *Nine's a Charm: Herbs of the Anglo-Saxon Healing Poem*

Heathenry for the Solitary Practitioner by Thea Prothero is a highly accessible and engaging book. The author's writing style is welcoming, thoughtful, and authentic, which invites the reader to a wealth of knowledge for solo practitioners. I also appreciated the real-life experiences Prothero shares. These stories are another invitation for those interested in Heathen practices who may have only heard of particular places and practices. With source text quotes, images, descriptions of rituals, altars, holidays, and resources, readers can build a practice that supports their Heathen journey.
Irisanya Moon, author of *The Norns: Weavers of Fate & Magick* and *Circe: Goddess of Sorcery*

I have and will always advocate for Heathens and Pagans to create, to share their perspective and knowledge. It's crucial in this sphere, especially as we have a tendency to be private and isolated in our individual practices. Here, then, Thea has collated a comprehensive guide that I'm sure will be an essential tool for those that hope to feel less alone in their path and journey. Elsewhere, the author has offered a concise summary of the foundational elements of Heathenry. We need more of this in the world, material that helps break down barriers and open the gates to those who are interested in learning more, but don't know where to start. An excellent read.
Sif Brookes, author of *Valkyrjur Servant or Master,* presenter of the *Heathen Hangour* podcast, and trustee of The Pagan Federation

I'm often asked for beginner's books on heathenry, or for something people can read to understand my religion. Whilst there are some great little books out there, I never feel they represent the norse paganism of today in the UK. And this is why I was so pleased to see Thea's book because it brings heathenry

right up to the here and now in a way that really resonates. It's fabulous to see so many voices within it, talking about their experiences, and especially welcome to hear women's voices. Thea's communication with Andy Pardy on extremism is also incredibly valuable as an important subject it would be easy to gloss over or shy away from. A recommended book.
Katie Gerrad, author of *Odin's Gateways and Seidr: The Gate Is Open*

I love this book. This book has captivated me to the extent that I found it impossible to set aside. I have read it three times, each time gaining valuable insights from this remarkable work. With every reading, I have emerged feeling fulfilled and have discovered new lessons within its pages. It serves as a comprehensive guide to Heathenry, a rapidly expanding polytheistic religious movement in northern Europe. The text delves into the cosmology, values, ethics, and contemporary rituals associated with this tradition. It serves as an excellent resource for solitary practitioners and is an ideal introduction for those interested in exploring heathenry. Thea, provides clear guidance on integrating these practices into daily life. Additionally, the inclusion of practical exercises encourages active engagement, making it a valuable resource for anyone looking to enhance their devotional practices. Highly recommended.
Kylie Holmes, author of *Pagan Portals-Runes, The Ancient Art of Tasseography: How to Read Tea Leaves and Coffee Grounds,* and *Journey with the Runes*

Heathenry for the Solitary Practitioner by Thea Prothero is an exciting, empowering, and extremely accessible guide to modern Heathenry, crafted with scholarship as well as personal insight. Blending ancient mythology with practical advice, Thea Prothero introduces readers to the essential elements of

Heathen belief systems, from cosmology and the gods to ritual and runic wisdom. Her personal journey into Heathenry adds intimacy and insight, making the book relatable and inspiring for anyone exploring or deepening their practice, particularly those drawn to a more solitary path. This brilliant book stands out for its balanced approach to history and spirituality, providing a well-researched framework that straddles yet deeply respects ancient traditions alongside more modern perspectives. Thea Prothero addresses the complexities of modern Heathenry with sensitivity and intelligence, encouraging inclusivity and thoughtful exploration of heritage. Richly informative yet grounded in everyday relevance, *Heathenry for the Solitary Practitioner* is an invaluable resource for anyone looking to connect with the Old Ways in a most profound and meaningful way.
Mab Jones, poet, editor, author of *Bog Witch,* and BBC Radio 4 Presenter

This book is an absolute delight. Thea Prothero provides a brief, yet thorough, introduction to Heathenry for the modern solitary practitioner. Our collective library has been lacking a book like this, which gives the reader a taste of history, lore, and practice. Thea's sense of humor shines through as well, which is a welcome antidote to the idea that Heathenry must be serious, stuffily academic, or stoic. The primer on the Gods and Goddesses is especially helpful, as is the guide to the Norse worldview and the discussion of the Runes. Heathenry provides more than enough to get a seeker started on this path, and plenty of guideposts for further exploration. Even those of us who are not Heathen ourselves, but who encounter seekers in our own communities, will benefit from keeping this book handy. This slim volume is fat with ideas and possibilities.
Susan Harper, PhD, feminist & author of *Pagan Portals-Feminist Witchcraft*

A refreshing, accessible, and intimate companion for anyone stepping onto the road of the solitary Heathen practitioner. The blend of research and personal accounts makes this a true treasure for your spiritual library.
Magin Rose, runic teacher & course leader

Pagan Portals

Heathenry for the Solitary Practitioner

Pagan Portals

Heathenry for the Solitary Practitioner

Thea Prothero

MOON BOOKS

London, UK

Washington, DC, USA

CollectiveInk

First published by Moon Books, 2026
Moon Books is an imprint of Collective Ink Ltd.,
Unit 11, Shepperton House, 89 Shepperton Road, London, N1 3DF
office@collectiveinkbooks.com
www.collectiveinkbooks.com
www.moon-books.net

For distributor details and how to order please visit the 'Ordering' section on our website.

ISBN: 978 1 80341 993 0
978 1 78904 930 5 (ebook)
Library of Congress Control Number: 2024950890

A CIP catalogue record for this book is available from the British Library.

Design: Lapiz Digital Services

UK: Printed and bound by CPI Group (UK) Ltd, Croydon, CR0 4YY
US: Printed and bound by Thomson-Shore, 7300 West Joy Road, Dexter, MI 48130

Contents

Acknowledgements

There have been so many generous folks who have helped me with this book: Firstly, my family and in particular my partner who has taken on extra work to enable me to spend time writing. I would like to thank the wonderful women who came forward to be interviewed about their Heathen practice; Sif, Pauline, Vikki, Natalia, Anna – and not forgetting the one man, Chris, a creator who was generous enough to answer questions about his work. To Andrew Pardy who generously lent me his expertise. The many, many people who have inspired me to write this book, authors, artists and Heathens! My publisher, and editor, Trevor Greenfield for your patience and belief in me.

And lastly to the gods – in particular, the one who wanders but is never lost.

Author's Note

I should like to point out that as this is an introductory book. I am currently studying for an MLitt in Viking Studies, so my predominant area of focus here is Norse Heathenry; although I would be remiss if I didn't also cover aspects of Anglo-Saxon Heathenry because where I live, I have been steeped in their history since I was a child, and their presence is very evident to me. If that isn't enough, I am an archaeology nerd, so you will find I use historical details to add context to most things. I refer regularly to the key texts – *The Poetic Edda, The Prose Edda* and various Sagas, usually Icelandic.

But in order for a tree to grow and flourish its roots need to be fed, and it's the same for faith – so in this book you will find references to modern movies, contemporary novels and even video games that re-imagine and sometimes push against some of the old-world views in Heathenry in new and exciting directions. Heathenry needs to be constantly evolving.

This work does not claim to be reconstructionist although it may use components from this type of Heathenry, and it definitely features UPG (Unverified Personal Gnosis).

As this is an introduction; it is meant as a stepping stone for anyone who is interested in Heathenry, especially if you are unable or simply don't want to work with others. It does not hold all the answers but will hopefully inspire you to seek out your own. Heathenry is sometimes described as the faith (or religion) with homework and this is your starting point.

Introduction

The Beginning

Early of ages
When nothing was.
There was neither sand nor sea
Nor cold waves.
The earth was not found
Nor the sky above.
Ginnungagap was there,
But grass, nowhere.
(Sturluson. Snorri. *Prose Edda*. 2005. p.12)

There was nothing, a void in space and time, a great gulf of blackness. This was Ginnungagap (The gaping abyss). To the north s of this vast emptiness was a land of ice called Niflheim and to the south a land of fire called Muspelheim. A great river ran through Niflheim and divided into twelve smaller rivers, each flowing into the abyss of Ginnungagap slowly over eons these rivers began to fill the great gulf with a huge frozen plane which grew ever closer to the fires of Muspelheim.

In due course, the volcanic drops of fire fell onto the ice plane and melted it, and from this the first primordial being was created; Ymir the first jötunn – frost giant. As he slept, he sweated and from his arm pit and from the flesh on his leg, gave birth to three more jötnar. These were the first beings.

From the ice and snow came another being, the great cow Audhumla, who fed the giants with her milk and licked salt from the rocks. After nearly three days of licking the rocks, she revealed the head of a being so beautiful and strong: the first god, Buri.

Buri was kind and good and looking about him, saw the jötnar as evil and cruel. Eons passed and from Buri sprang Bor, his son, who wedded a giantess called Bestla, and therefore mixing the races of jötnar and god. They in time, had three children; Óðinn, Vili, and Ve. (Other stories name then as Óðinn, Hoenir and Lodurr, which I will examine later in the Gods chapter).

After ions of time had passed, Óðinn and His brothers grew older. They could not live in the world of Niflheim with its ice or in the world of Muspelheim where they would burn. They knew that the giants, especially Ymir was a threat to their existence, and were their natural enemies. The brothers decided to destroy Ymir.

When the deed was done, salty grey blood poured from the giant in vast quantities which formed the seas. The soil was created by Óðinn and his brothers from Ymir's flesh and his bones became the mountains. Rocks were formed from Ymir's teeth. When you look into the sky, this is the inside of Ymir's massive skull. The stars and planets are flashes of the fires from Muspelheim, and clouds are bits of Ymir's brain.

To keep the giants at bay, Óðinn, and his brother's used Ymir's eyebrows to form a vast wall that surrounds the middle of the world, a place known as Midgard....

All mythologies have a creation story. All beliefs begin somewhere, so the Norse creation story is a good a place to introduce a book on Heathenry for the solitary practitioner. Of course, the story continues with the further creation of the world, of humankind and the other realms and beings. All of this can be found in the Voluspa, the Seeress's prophecy, the first offering in the *Poetic Edda*.

Modern Heathenry is basically a reconstruction of ancient Northen European religion and beliefs. The original Heathens were pre-Christian and lived over a thousand years ago in areas around the North Sea. This included Scandinavia, Anglo-Saxon England, Germany, parts of Scotland, and Ireland, Friesland, and Jutland.

Today, Heathens exist around the world, reviving and interpreting these ancient beliefs, all of which derive from archaeological data, the Eddas, Sagas and Anglo-Saxon poems. Many people today follow the Heathen worldview, (I like this term far better than calling Heathenry a religion, with all its associated dogma and connotations) either in groups, sometimes called kindreds, through organisations such as Asatru UK, or individually, like myself.

I came to Heathenry in a very round about fashion: when I was a child, I read *The Hobbit* by JRR Tolkien which was, not only a fantastic adventure story heavily steeped in Old Norse and Germanic tales and myths, but my introduction to Runes. Seeing them on the page both intrigued and fascinated me. Tolkien's explanation of Runes at the beginning of the book, although simplistic, gave them credence and presented a whole history that was unknown to me and a stepping stone into a new world. To say I was drawn to the Runes is an understatement! At an age when I was unsure of everything, and my world regularly turned upside down, they seemed to offer me clarity and steadfastness. I found I could naturally intuit meaning with very little guidance. The Runes spoke to me.

Over the years since, I created my own sets to bring about stability when crises came, (and many did) they offered a clear voice of reason when I needed them. I put them aside to study and practice other spiritualities, and for a time, these sufficed, and I made do. Increasingly though, the philosophical aspects of their teachings seemed too far removed from my life and I felt as though I was simply mouthing words to prayers, I didn't feel any connection to. I needed a belief system that would challenge me, push me beyond anything I'd known before, and that would never stop teaching me to see the world in new multiple nuanced ways. It was at this time I noticed a grey shadow of a person had begun appearing in my meditations and dreams. At first, I thought it was a misinterpretation, a ghost perhaps.

Slowly He solidified, but He wasn't pushy or demanding and I largely ignored Him.

This all changed on the day I visited Grimes Graves in Norfolk. This is a neolithic flint mine, which was re-named during the Anglo-Saxon period after their god Grim (which means masked or hidden one) and is another name for Woden (Odin). I had recently made a new set of Runes from sacred stone and decided to bring them with me that day. I cast them on the ground near to one of the infilled mineshafts and concentrated. It was not the ground that I had cast onto, but a shadowy hand. "Not now" was all I heard.

That night I dreamt of the grey figure in the mine shaft at Grimes Graves, his face was covered by a large hat, and he carried a staff of wood that seemed to climb into the clouds. He led me to a vast cavernous wooden cave made of tree root, which twisted and enclosed everything around it. On one of these vast roots, carved in rudimentary Runes, was my name, and the roots seemed to all point towards the figure. I knew who He was. I was afraid.

A year before this point, I had read the rather excellent introduction to Odin by Morgan Daimler, and following her advice, was rather wary of working with him. I also had a somewhat distorted image of Heathery as a very male dominated belief system. However, I participated in some online courses and rituals before and during Lockdown, with some brilliant Heathen teachers, who restored my faith in trusting my instincts, believing in my own personal gnosis.

I am a Heathen, and if you have picked up or bought this book, I am thinking you might be interested in Heathenry too.

So why a book for a solitary practitioner? I am one, that is to say, I am one – largely. I do belong remotely to several organisations, and have taken part in Heathen rituals, which are described later in this book. But there are two reasons I am solitary; firstly, because I don't live anywhere near any Heathen kindreds or groups, so it makes it nearly impossible to attend meetings or rituals; secondly, I prefer to do my own thing, at my own pace and have control over how and when I practice my faith. If I want to work with others, then I can, albeit because of the aforementioned geographical issue, remotely.

Something that is very prominent in modern consciousness and social media, and which I will go into more detail in the last chapter, is Heathenry and far right extremism. Just because the original Norse people and their faith came from northern Europe, has no bearing on who can be a Heathen. I strongly believe the Gods don't care about these issues; it is far beneath them. They choose whoever they want, and answer prayers when they want to, or not, regardless of who is asking. I know that the organisations and individuals I have contact with are all inclusive. As Asatru UK say on their website: *"We strongly believe in frith, in respect, in respecting others in open mindedness..."*

So, while we're on the subject of controversy, Let's start as we mean to go on and examine two subjects that can be considered contentious. These words have caused arguments and mayhem whenever they're mentioned in relation to Heathenry: Women & Vikings!

Chapter 1

Heathen Women

A common misconception within popular culture is that Heathenry is aimed at and intended for men. You could be, to some extent, forgiven for thinking this – it's hard not to be swayed by social media and popular entertainment depictions of Heathens as either hyper masculine, or head banging heavy metal fans. Your ideas could originate from Victorian heroic denotations of Vikings, which pretty much offered the pervasive ideal until more recently. On first appearances, it appears that the Eddas largely concentrate on what men get up to and this is largely true, however, the women that are mentioned usually have an important role within the storyline. Often the women mentioned are consulted on matters of politics and warfare, such as the character Ragna in the *Orkneyinga Saga,* who owns and runs a farm on North Ronaldsay and is described as "...an intelligent woman..." (p.128). She is mentioned several times, and her opinion is sought by the Earl regarding his political allies.

Within the *Saga of the Greenlanders* and the *Saga of Erik The Red,* we learn of Gudrid Thorbjanardottir, who grew up in Iceland, settled in Greenland and went on an expedition with her husband and settled in Vinland (Newfoundland in Canada). Here, she had a child, and although the settlement didn't last very long, her achievement, for a woman at that time, was remarkable. It is notable that when she was younger, she was called a *"skorunger"*, which literally means a fire-poker, a metaphorical name for a woman who is assertive and who has leadership qualities.

And Let's not forget that in The Voluspa, Odin – the head god, the leader of all, has gone to great lengths to awaken a dead Volva – a seeress – to get the answers he needs. He could not get these answers without her help. That is extremely significant. The Nornir, weavers of fate, control the destiny of all, including gods. None can escape their fate which is woven by these supernatural female beings. Freya, the mighty Vanir goddess has jurisdiction over the battle dead, even before Odin. She taught Seidr, (magic) to the Aesir gods and importantly has agency over her own sexuality.

If we consider Norse female archetypes within popular culture, the one is constantly recurring is the shieldmaiden. From the TV series *Vikings*, Lagatha is considered a great warrior, known to be both wise and battle savvy; she is also mother to Bjorn Ironside who is a fearsome warrior, a homemaker and farmer. Within literature, the character Eowyn from *Lord of The Rings* by J.R.R. Tolkien, describes herself, and is described by others, as a shieldmaiden. There is strong historical evidence for female warriors; sometimes causing a degree of controversy; Birka grave BJ 581, one of the best known and infamous Viking graves found in Sweden, was for years considered to be that of a warrior man. This is not surprising, if we consider it was first excavated in the late Victorian Age. The grave was large, filled with weapons, horses and gaming pieces, and the skeleton was tall in stature – so, of course, it was a Viking man, right? In 2017 the results of the DNA analysis revealed two X chromosomes, meaning this was a woman. This has led to a reassessment of how Viking society is viewed. We can now, therefore, confidently say that women were leaders, and warriors too.

Historically, who could fail to be impressed by the most famous ship burial ever discovered in the world: the Oseberg Ship which was the pride of the Viking Ship Museum in Oslo. This lavish burial discovered near Tonsberg in Norway in 1904, with the ship and burial dating from approx. 834 CE. Inside the ship were two bodies, both women, both laid out on the same bed. One was aged around eighty years old at death, the other was in her fifties. The amount of grave goods and their opulence suggests this was a very high-status burial. Over the years, many theories were proposed; that one of the women was perhaps a queen, another, was that one was a Volva, or possibly a shaman. These hypotheses can never be proved, and we shall never know for sure who they were. That they were both women who lived to good ages for that time in history, obviously had money, and indeed were buried in such an impressive ship is highly significant. They clearly had agency over their own wealth and were respected by their community, proven by the very nature of their impressive burial.

It's all very well looking at the past, but what is the current situation for women in Heathenry? To give a broader prospective on being a Heathen woman in today's world, I asked several women if they could describe their Heathen practice to me and give me an overview of their experience of being a modern Heathen woman.

Sif is an author and active member of Asatru UK as well as the Pagan Federation. She lives in the North of England.

I began by asking her how she discovered Heathenry:

> *I've been Heathen now for over seven years, and prior to that, I was a very ardent Atheist. The nihilistic sort who used to believe that there was nothing after life, and people were a little silly for believing in anything else. I held a 'live and let live' approach – never to the degree of being Anti-theist, of course. Saying that, I've always been incredibly fascinated by Greek and Nordic mythology and found myself particularly interested in the ritualistic and religious side of it in terms of the realities of practice. From my early twenties I gradually became more interested in researching Pre-Christian Germanic animistic practices including Heathenry (which I was surprised had a modern day following!) until one day it was like a switch flipped in my head. "This feels right. This feels good. I feel*

more whole". Within a few months of further research, I had moved from a mindset of "the Gods are aspects" to "the Gods are real and living". It all happened very quickly at that point.

There was also the feeling of 'coming home' which you hear many Heathens talk about, and that was very much the case for me. I had a rather potent experience in relation to Freyja, who I was drawn to very early on in my path, and then another equally evocative experience from Sif which was very unexpected. I haven't looked back since.

Sif went on to tell me how she practices her Heathenry:

I take a reconstructionist perspective to my flavour of Heathenry, which I think comes from my original fascination and my Atheist background. I like knowing that what I'm doing has some sort of historical precedence...I guess 'tested' precedence. I also enjoy that innate connection to the past that is touched by the reconstructionist approach, that you may be saying the same words / the same intention and taking the same steps of those in the past. There is a spiritual echo there that helps inform my own practice, an ancestral link even if it is a little muddy from a thousand-year gap and various veils of obfuscation.

She continues in more detail:

My practice is pretty bare bones ...! I tend to keep things rather minimalistic, with the exception of weaponry and armour, and various other trinkets. My house and religious space is peppered with spears, swords and axes. I find the act of maintaining them very meditative and it helps me ground and connect with the Gods I worship. Devotional acts are also important to me, and I'm currently growing out my hair in honour of Sif (I have had it shaved and short for a very long time!)

I wanted to know if Sif had a primary deity:

> *I imagine from the outset, many people who know me would expect me to say the Valkyries.* (Sif has just written a book about them.) *I adore the Valkyries, and they absolutely do play a huge role in my practice. The main deities I worship are the Valkyries, alongside Freyja, Hel, Sif, Skadi, Angrboda, Ran – and, of course, all of the others including and especially the jötnar. I strongly believe that Sif herself has jötunn heritage if not being a jötunn herself, and she is another example of one of the jötnar being integrated into the Aesir. For me, she is an understated strength, potent – the quiet calm in the centre of the storm. She's a goddess that always 'has my back' when I'm at my lowest and reminds me of my own inner strength. Ultimately, I can't really pick a primary deity, as all of my practice is interlaced and interconnected by death deities, and their role in feeding into life. The Valkyries are a focal point, but not I would say an outright 'favourite'.*

I asked Sif how she feels being a woman and a Heathen: I wanted to know if she had ever experienced any issues because of it:

> *I feel, often counter to popular belief, that Heathenry is very empowering as a woman. Misconceptions abound, of course, but we're still very much in the process of realising the importance of women when it came to religious and cultural practices in the late Iron Age. There are incredibly strong women and feminine forces within Heathenry – Frigg, Sif, Freyja, the Valkyries, Hel, the Nornir, Sol, and so on – that act as inspirations and drivers for personal improvement. They drive me to be better.*
>
> *As a woman who isn't the most stereotypically feminine in the way I present, I also find significant comfort in the blurred boundaries when it comes to many of these goddesses and their*

presentations. They wear armour and wield weapons, and they don't bend to social conventions of the Viking Age or ours. They thrive in spaces that are deemed to be masculine – the battlefield, life and death.

Of course, there exists the flip side of all of this, and that's where my own issues lie. There exist certain groups that believe that women are secondary to men, and they see Heathenry as this monolith that absolutely enforces their beliefs. They ignore the Goddesses and their power and reduce their importance. They see the Valkyries as mere personal wights, mead maidens, servants. There's a deliberate effort to put the Goddesses into boxes they don't belong, into subservient positions. They see women within Heathenry as almost deviant and uphold the macho uber-masculinity of the outdated image of the Viking Age as the ultimate truth. Naturally, I can't stand that perspective and speaks to a lack of knowledge of the period and the literature.

Pauline is a solitary Heathen, living in Scotland, with a young family. Below she describes how she discovered Heathenry to me:

I can't actually remember (When I became Heathen). I learnt about paganism in my late teens and I think I did a bit of reading on the various paths back then although I didn't consider myself as Pagan until my mid-twenties. For a long time my path was Druidry and I thought of Heathen deities as the party next door, nice enough but not my thing. Then Loki decided to come knocking at my door and I let Him in.

I asked Pauline if she could elaborate a little on her relationship with Loki?

I have a pendant for Loki and a statue in my altar. I offer him drinks, usually alcohol on Saturdays and I regularly chat to him. I find him incredibly supportive of the challenges of being a parent to unique kids as well as supportive when I feel misunderstood. One of my tattoos has a stylised form of his name in a sigil designed for me and I've also offered my pain to him during more painful tattoo sessions. I've journeyed to Kirkby Stephen to see the Loki stone there three times now, once prompted to do so before the spring equinox in 2020. We visited about a week or two before the first major lockdown.

Pauline told me how she practices her Heathenry:

I talk about the stories with my kids and my lad is now Heathen too. I have a personal altar I make offerings of liquid, often alcohol, at and sit in front of and commune with deities. I also devote some of my spinning and weaving time to Frigg. I think of volunteering in online groups as a form of service too. Oh, I have a couple of personal prayers and chants that I use too.

I have runes. They sit on my altar. Sometimes I use them for full readings for others but mostly I stir the shallow bowl I keep them in to see of one or two falls out at least once a week while asking deities if they have any particular guidance for me. Sometimes the time has an obvious meaning for the next few days, sometimes the meaning becomes clearer as time passes. I also have Godposts on my altar, devotional jewellery that I change each day and designated little bowls and goblets for offerings.

My personal practice is very simple. I rarely cast circles or call directions even though my path is Druid and Heathen. The different paths are mainly reflected in the deities I honour.

Why are you a solitary Heathen?

I'm solitary in terms of physical practice because I want to be. I've done face to face group things in the past, facilitated a Druid group for a while. I'm happy doing my own thing now.

Pauline told me how she feels her experiences being a Heathen woman in today's society:

> *Male voices seem to dominate strongly in many Heathen spaces. There also seems to be a media driven idea that many Heathen women are sexy young warrior types or subservient home types. I'm neither. I haven't had any major issues. I am a member of Heathen Women United. (an online group specifically for women).*

Viki is a Solitary Heathen from the UK.

How did you come to be a Heathen?

> *My first exposure to Heathen ideas was on a Yahoo e-group back around 2000-2003. It was a mixed pagan group that included people who became leaders within their own paths. The conversations were intelligent and wide-ranging. One was about concepts such as karma and wyrd. Wyrd fitted right with me, and I started looking for more. I must have been in contact with a Heathen with a lot of experience around this time, as we had a drink after work one night. I was working in Nottingham at the time, and she in Sheffield. I joined her new email group for Heathens and a rough-camping holiday weekend in the New Forest for pagans. They invited me to join the kingroup.*
>
> *Back then, there were few Heathens and fewer kingroups. Most of us met online. Our core kingroup included two of the leading Heathens at the time, about a half a dozen others, a Brythonic Celtic reconstructionist and two Roman Religio. We also had others who joined us from time to time, including a leading Celtic recon and a shaman. I learnt about Heathenry from my kingroup, from reading the Eddas and talking to Heathens online.*

However, the important event wasn't an idea of meeting the kingroup. The push came from a god who came into my life. He was a god associated with Heathenry and he came sometime after that first meeting with others. I can't recall when or how he announced itself which is extraordinary for someone who was so important to me for a few years. I can remember all the others. I certainly remember asking (after a few years) whether he wanted to oath to him. Within Heathenry in the UK at that time, oathing was taken very seriously and an oath to that god, even more so. He surprised me again by refusing. He said (in effect) 'there's someone coming with more right to you.'

Now, the trouble with the god who came was that he blew apart my lovely hard-polytheist-every-god-is-separate ideology. He's happy to take several names. I didn't like the usual one, so we agreed on Mr Forester.

What is your personal practice like?

I've accumulated a relationship with a few gods over the years, when writing novels. The books where I explored other pagan religions were always done by seeing if any of the gods associated with that culture would talk to me. As a result, I have one room in my house devoted to gods and ancestors, which contains images of some of them. I don't have images of Heathen gods I've had no dealings with, and (oddly for a Heathen but not uniquely) I avoid Odhinn. My friends who are oathed to Odhinn always offer to Loki as well (per the relevant text, which I can't recall just now), and I would happily offer to Odhinn in their houses. Not in mine.

In general, I talk to three gods every day: Loki, Freyja and Mr Forester. I have images or tokens of them on my main altar and in my bedroom. The main altar is on my upstairs landing, and I don't go to bed without stopping to talk to them.

My other daily practice is to say Sigdrifa's Paryer as a toast in the evening. Other timed practices are full moon (to gods and wights, except Hel) and dark moon (to Hel and ancestors). Non-timed practical relationships are by subject: the garden belongs to Mr F, home textiles and design to Freyja, and a mixed bag to Loki – computers, journeys and writing.

I have a special prayer for the ancestors, as I found it very difficult to find a way to relate to them, and the prayer is my answer.

I asked Viki how she felt about being a woman and a Heathen and whether this had ever caused her any issues:

I came across prejudice before I was a Heathen, but never encountered it as a Heathen. It's never occurred to me to consider there's any gender difference. I was an anti-discrimination para-legal for years, so I tend to be sensitive to harassment or discrimination of protected groups, for example, gender. That's not to say it doesn't exist, only that I have not experienced anything.

Vikki was keen to give advice to new Heathens:

Talk to the wights and the gods. Watch nature and get used to its rhythms, as it's the world of the wights and the old Heathen cultures. Look for inclusive (pro-diversity) groups. Read the Eddas. Read the Sagas. Be aware of the source of things because if you don't know what's Heathen and what's not, you'll be a sucker for misinformation.*

Natalia is a solitary Heathen from Southeast Asia, who enjoys travelling all over the world.

She found Heathenry as I did, through her love of Tolkien and Runes:

I was first and foremost a Tolkien fan during my adolescence and wanted to learn Old Norse because of it. This led me down a mythological rabbit hole, and I soon became familiar with the Gods and sagas. I was an atheist for many years but started wearing a Mjølnir pendant when I was 18 for some reason I still don't know. I eventually turned to Heathenry proper at around 23-24, when I faced some really traumatic life events and had a spiritual crisis, and never looked back.

She tells me about her Heathen practice:

I'm a solitary practitioner but hosted my first blot ceremony among close friends for winter solstice 2023. I work primarily with runes and cards (including tarot, but not my favourite). During special events I often say a prayer or give offerings, but I have to say that I am quite lazy and forgetful I bless my ritual circle by passing around it with palo santo and/or sage nine times before drawing a sun cross over it. I then bless it with mead. This is totally UPG but I've been doing it for a while. I then close the ritual circle the same way after rituals

I asked her if there was a reason she was a solitary practitioner:

It's mostly a preference. I'm a member of Asatru UK (AUK) but don't attend their events or interact with members aside from online. I just prefer to keep my religion to myself, and the way I practice (blood magic) isn't for everyone.

Tal tells me about her Runic practice and her pain offerings to the gods:

Runes are my primary divination tool; I am also a hook/ body suspension practitioner and member of the Church of Pain and dedicate my body in blood sacrifice to the Gods. My

> *offerings have been accepted and I'm very grateful to be able to practice hook suspension with fellow practitioners in Norway. I use hooks and blood in my suspension rituals, as well as other components that vary – my most recent suspension included roses and love letters from an ex, as well as mugwort, chamomile, holly, wild mushrooms, and lichen for the Gods I was sacrificing to*

I inquired about how Natalia felt being a Heathen woman and whether she had faced any problems because of this:

> *Not at all, nobody has ever treated me differently for being a woman and a large number of my Heathen friends are men!*

Interestingly, the consensus here from the women I spoke to, who come from all walks of life, and all have their own unique ways of practicing their Heathenry, is that they have not had any issues or been actively discriminated against, being a Heathen woman. This supports the inclusive agenda within modern Heathenry.

Chapter 2

The V word

I guarantee that if you happen to introduce the word 'Viking' into any conversation, discussion or debate on social media, you will release a massive bone of contention that's even too big for Fenrir the Wolf to munch on!

Joking aside, the question I am going to examine is whether it is acceptable to use the word Viking when referring to the 8th-11th Century Nordic people from what is now Scandinavia.

For a long time, this umbrella term was used to describe anyone; from the vicious raiders who invaded parts of Britian, taking slaves and generally causing trouble, like in *The Last Kingdom* TV series, to the peaceful and loving families in *How to Train Your Dragon* films and books. They were all Vikings.

The origin of the word Viking may come from the Old Norse word, *Vikingr,* which means 'raider' but could also indicate a person who participated in expeditions. Some scholars, however, find this label too restrictive and have suggested it could simply relate to a traveller, someone who travelled away from their homelands. Others have posited that the root word *Vikja* means 'to travel by sea.' Indeed, it could originally simply have referred to a geographical area in western Norway.

In England during the 8-11th centuries, the Scandinavian invaders were simply called 'Danes' whether they came from Denmark or not. The more derogatory word *Viking* began to appear in the later Icelandic sagas, referring to ill-tempered pirates, who were presented as a menace to the then modern and civilised (i.e. Christian) Icelandic society.

During the 18th and 19th centuries, Vikings were reimagined in a more romantic light during the Viking Revival when the tales of the Vikings were portrayed in a wholly heroic way.

Wagner's famous *Der Ring des Nibelungen* – Ring Cycle Opera, which was based on the tragic story of Brunhild, a Valkyrie, and her lover, Sigurd the dragon slayer, was met with huge critical acclaim. The American poet, Henry Wadsworth Longfellow released many poems based around Norse mythology during the late Victorian era, which lead to a cascade of interest in all things Viking. Even today Viking is still a blanket term to describe anyone and anything from Nordic culture.

So, should we use the word 'Viking' today? And if so, what should we be referring to?

Whilst it's true that Viking in its original form does refer to a person's role or activity in society, rather than an ethnic group, and it can intimate that all Nordic people from that time, were marauding pirates who terrorized other nations, I think we are doing the people – the Vikings if you will – an injustice by only identifying negative associations. The word Viking has become integrated into many modern languages; and further, when I posed this question to Scandinavian friends, the general consensus was that the Viking age is considered in a fairly neutral or positive light, reflecting on the exploration and skill shown by these early navigators and explorers and that that they were brave, skilled and strong warriors. Some even considered that being called a Viking nowadays, would be a compliment.

Personally, I think it's up to the individual if they wish to use the word Viking or the term Viking Age or not. I am going to be using the word Viking throughout this book, starting with a quick look at the history of the Vikings now.

There are many, many books about the Viking Age, and history, so I am only going to offer a brief overview here, enough (I hope) to whet your appetite and encourage you to find out more.

Although not the first raid in England, The most recognisable early record of the Vikings in England was their famous sacking of Lindisfarne Priory in 793 CE[1]. This attack sent shockwaves through the Christian Anglo-Saxon kingdoms because they attacked a holy site of unprotected and peaceful men. There were almost certainly earlier, perhaps unsuccessful, attacks around Great Britain, but Lindisfarne was considered the main catalyst.

During the next century, the Anglo-Saxon kingdoms paid huge sums of what is called Danegeld[2] to would-be raiders in an attempt to stop the attacks. In 865 CE the Great Heathen Army[3] invaded England via East Anglia, and the campaign of invasion lasted many years. In 867 CE Viking armies managed to capture the mighty town of York, and from this point, vast areas of England became Viking. In 886 King Alfred, ruler and king of Wessex – one of the only areas of the country that remained Anglo-Saxon – brokered a peace treaty, which denoted everything in the north of the country was Viking owned, these areas were known as the Danelaw[4].

These areas were extensively settled by the Vikings; however, the peace treaty was dissolved in 954 CE, and the culmination of centuries of Viking invasions came after the Anglo-Saxon king Aethelred the Unready foolishly decreed that all Danes living in his part of England should be killed, leading to the St. Brice's Day massacre in 1002 CE[5]. These actions directly lead to Sweyn Forkbeard's invasion of England, which meant he became king in 1013 CE[6].

There followed a remarkable and unprecedented time in British history: Cnut The Great[7], son of Forkbeard, ruled the country as part of a larger North Sea Empire, which included present day Denmark, Norway and parts of Sweden, he was also overlord of The Northern Isles, parts of Scotland, the Hebrides and parts of Ireland.

The Vikings were exemplary tradespeople who travelled far and wide including the Volga Trade routes in present day Russia, Belarus and the Ukraine. Known as the Rus[8], (after whom Russia is named). they even formed an elite bodyguard for numerous Byzantian emperors, known as the Varangian Guard[9]. Out of interest, if you happen to be lucky enough to visit the Hagia-Sofia Mosque in Istanbul, Turkey, and look carefully enough you may one or possibly two, Runic graffiti carvings on the marble parapets.

Most, if not all, cultures have a dark history, and the Vikings are no exception. One of the 'commodities' that the Vikings traded with the Ottoman and Byzantine empires were slaves[10], indeed, the slave trade was the biggest business for the Viking conquerors of Ireland and other places. The Vikings were slavers; they actively kidnapped and enslaved their conquered lands, then either sold or traded any they didn't want. This is a vast dark spot on Viking history, and I am not going to downplay how significant it was. To put it in context, however, many, many people and so-called civilisations all over the word relied on slavery for wealth and work.

The Viking longship[11] is probably the most iconic representation of the Vikings, even today. These ships were sleek, narrow and light, making them easier to transport over land when needed. The shallow draft hull allowed the ships to be speedy and able to traverse waters only one meter deep. A fine example of the longship is the Oseberg ship in the Norwegian ship museum.

It was a longship that sailed all the way to Newfoundland on the Canadian coast, from Greenland in the 10th century[12]. According to the Icelandic Sagas, it was Erik the Red's son, Leif Eriksson, who first discovered Vinland when his ship was blown off course. Here they created a short-term settlement, before returning to Greenland. The Settlment in Greenland lasted for nearly 500 years before being abandoned.

The Viking Age began to start to decline after their assimilation into Christianity which had begun to take root in the 11th century[13]. Many royal dynasties were legitimised by the Catholic church, leading to a change in the aspiration of the peoples, along with new laws on slavery and raiding.

The most prominent and lasting legacy of the Vikings is evident in the English language where 139 words that are part of the core vocabulary, such as *leg* and *egg*. – typically, words starting with 'sk'- are Scandinavian in origin.[14]

Another important legacy of the Vikings is their spirituality, which today is known as Heathenry or Asatru.[15]

Notes:

1 There is considerable reference to the attack on Lindisfarne and its date. In this instance, please refer to pages 26-28 of *Viking Britian* by Thomas Williams and page 271 of The *Children of Ash & Elm* by Neil Price.

2 Danegeld literally meant "Danish yield" in Anglo-Saxon. It was raised to pay off Viking raiders in order to stop them ravaging the Anglo-Saxon kingdoms. An excellent example can be found on page 89 of *River Kings* by Cat Jarman,

3 The Great Heathen Army was a coalition of Scandinavian kings and warriors who massed together and invaded Britain from East Anglia and aimed to conquer all the Anglo-Saxon kingdoms.

4 Danelaw, for more information on the treaty, please see pages 31-3 of *The Vikings in England, Settlement Society and Culture* by D. Hadley. Please also see the chapter on Danelaw (page 210 – in *Viking Britain* by Thomas Williams.

5 St Brice's Day Massacre for more information about the archaeological finds, please see page 286-9 in by Cat Jarman. and *Crypt by* Alice Roberts.

6 For more information about Sweyn Forkbeard as ruler of England please see (p. 323ff) *Viking Britain* by Thomas Williams.

7 King Cnut is the greatest unsung monarch of the UK in my opinion and a rather excellent book about Cnut is: King Cnut and the Viking Conquest of England 1016 by W.B. Bartlett. (Amberley Publishing. 2018. ISBN: 9781445682891

8 For more information on the Rus please see page 368-72 *Children of Ash & Elm by* Neil Price.

9 For more information on the Varangian Guard and the Runic markings in the Hagia-Sofia Mosque please see pages 428ff- of *Children of Ash & Elm* by Neil Price.

10 One of the most profound Viking artifacts found in Dublin Ireland is a metal shackle used to secure slaves together by the neck. Please see The Pursuit of Liberty in *Children of Ash & Elm* by Neil Price.

11 A great chapter about the history and development of Viking ships is Sea Steeds, page73ff in *River Kings* by Cat Jarman. Also, I would recommend visiting the Viking Ship Museum in Roskilde Denmark, for more information check out their website: https://www.vikingeskibsmuseet.dk/

12 For more information about the Viking settlements in North America please see page 493-4 of *Children of Ash & Elm* by Neil Price and, of course, The Greenland & Vinland *Sagas of Erik the Red*.

13 For information on the Christianisation of the Vikings please see pages 161-2 *The Conversion of Scandinavia: Vikings, Merchants, and Missionaries in the Remaking of Northern Europe* by Anders Winroth.

14 For more information on Viking words in the English language please see: https://www.babbel.com/en/magazine/139-norse-words.

15 For more information on Heathen organisations please see the Homework section at the back of the book.

Chapter 3

History in Reverse – The Anglo-Saxons

The Angles, Jutes and Saxons began arriving in England around 410 CE[1] during a time called The Dark Ages. Britian was in a state of flux caused by the Romans leaving from around 400 CE. There was a breakdown in society law became obsolete, and if any order remained, it was scattered and disorganised. The country was chaotic. This anarchic state offered a perfect opportunity for raiders, invaders and ultimately settlers.[2]

When the Anglo-Saxons – as their cultural identity eventually became – came over, they were pagan and followed a broadly similar pantheon to their younger and somewhat more well-known cousins, the Vikings.[3] Relatively quickly, the country was divided into separate kingdoms, starting in the south and east,[4] although there is some contention about the speed, scale and nature of these settlements. Was it a peaceful takeover? Or, was it a brutal invasion? One piece of evidence – a mass migration of the Britons into Brittany, France, would suggest the scale was immense.[5] It was reported that by 430 CE evidence of Roman material culture had all but disappeared and was completely replaced by Anglo-Saxon.

By the end of the 6th century, leaders of the now well-established kingdoms began to be considered kings, and in 565 CE Columba, a monk from Christian Ireland, arrived on Iona and created the now famous religious community which had widespread Celtic Christian influence upon the kingdoms around it. After Columba died, Augustine, chosen by the Pope Gregory The Great, landed on the isle of Thanet in Kent and proceeded to try and convert the pagan Anglo-Saxon kingdoms.[6]

The time of the Anglo-Saxons ended with the Battle of Hastings in 1066 CE. In their nearly 600-year tenure of England, they introduced writing, education and a legal system. The country was for part of the time unified against the raiding Vikings under Alfred The Great. Bede's *Ecclesiastical History of the English People,* written in 731 CE, gives a relatively contemporary account of the country from the Roman invasion until height of the Anglo-Saxons. Although presented from a Christian perspective, it is remarkable because it was a written book and a document of history.[7] The *Anglo-Saxon Chronicle* was probably created in the 9th Century and offers a relatively clear chronological history of the Anglo-Saxons and includes many details that were unrecorded elsewhere.[8]

Notes:

1 According to the Latin text the *Chronica Gallicia,* Britain was ravaged by Saxon invaders around 409-10 CE. For more information please see page 104 of *The Anglo-Saxon World,* by Nicholas Higham and Martin Ryan.

2 For more information about this time, please see *The Anglo-Saxons* by. Marc Morris.

3 For more information on the pagan Anglo-Saxons please see pages 36-40 of *The Anglo-Saxons* by Marc Morris. and *Rites and Religions of the Anglo-Saxons* by Gale Owen-Crocker.

4 For more information about the early Anglo-Saxon kingdoms please see page 2ff *An English Empire: Bede and the Early Anglo-Saxon Kings by* Nicholas Higham.

5 Was it a peaceful invasion or a hostile take-over? Please read the postscript on page 295 onwards in *Buried* by Alice Roberts.

6 For more information on the Anglo-Saxon conversion to Christianity please see *The Anglo-Saxons* by Marc Morris.

7 Please see *Ecclesiastical History books I, II, and III* edited by John Allen Giles (1843. Whittaker & Co. London).

8 I recommend Michael Swanton's *The Anglo-Saxon Chronicle.*

Chapter 4

Cosmology

In this chapter I am going to offer some key aspects from mythology that will help you begin to understand how the Norse people viewed their world. This will predominantly focus on the Norse perspective, simply because of the abundance of available material, although I will touch upon Anglo-Saxon belief relating to Wyrd.

Considering the cosmology of the Norse people helps us appreciate how they perceived the world around them, which in turn, enables us to piece everything we cognate about them into a strong framework of understanding. Or as Morgan Daimler explains succinctly: *"like a piece of a puzzle which by itself only offers us a small glimpse at the bigger picture they all form together."* (2022. p.13)

Creation

In the introduction to this book, I told of the beginning of time in Norse myth, starting with Ginnungagap, (the great void) with a quote from the *Prose Edda*. Continuing from that point in time – Odin and his brothers had killed the first primordial being, the *jötunn*, Ymir, and used his body to create the worlds. From Ymir's rotting corpse, they began to fashion the first living beings in the new worlds; from maggots came dwarves, one of each was placed at the four corners of Ymir's skull – the sky, and to this day they support it above our heads. The dwarves were named Austri, (East) Sudri, (South) Vestri, (West) and Nordri, (North). Later the gods found two driftwood tree trunks on the beach, they created two humans, a man from ash (Ask) and a woman from Elm (Embla).

The Nine Worlds

In Norse mythology there are nine worlds. Incidentally, the number nine in Norse mythology, is a sacred and reoccurring number, appearing on many occasions, for instance: Odin hung from the World Tree for nine days and nights, and Heimdall has nine mothers.

We know, at the beginning of time there were already two worlds, Niflheim in the north and Muspelheim in the south (with Ginnungagap between them). Both of these worlds are forces of nature: Niflheim is the frozen land, of ice, snow, glaciers, and tundra, similar to the North Pole and the north of the Scandinavian lands. Whereas Muspelheim in the south, is fiery hot, full of active volcanoes and in the south. Surt, the fire giant at the centre of Ragnarök, who, with his sword of fire, will slay Frey, lives in Muspelheim.

Midgard – middle world, and possibly middle earth in Tolkien's sagas, is where humans live and was created by Odin and his brothers from Ymir's body. It is our world, and the most familiar to us.

Asgard is the home of the Aesir, (and latterly, some of the Vanir) gods. I expect most of you are familiar with this realm. It is reachable by travelling along the Bifrost which is guarded by Heimdall. Most of the gods have halls here.

Vanaheim is the realm or world of the Vanir gods, and where Njord, Frey and Freya originally come from. There is not much information about Vanaheim, other than Njord returns there after Ragnarök.

Jotunheim is the world of the giants or *jötnar,* who lived after the death of Ymir and survived the river of blood which killed most of their kin. Thor regularly travels there to kill giants, and quite a few myths feature this world.

Ljosalfheim or Alfheim, is interestingly owned by Frey (as mentioned previously) and where the Alfar or Elves live. The

Alfar and their world is not featured in the myths but could be connected to the Landvaettir or land spirits and the Vanir.

Svartalfheim is the home of the dwarves. Svart means dark or even black could indicate that the dwarves live in caves or dark places underground. The dwarves who feature in the myths are usually smiths or great craftsmen.

Helheim is the dwelling place of most of the ancestors, and Hel the goddess of the dead. The afterlife is slightly more complicated as those who die in battle will go to Valhalla, or Sessrumnir and those who die at sea or by drowning will go to Ran's hall. I think it's fair to say, most of the ancestors will go to Helheim. Helheim is completely different than the Christian "Hell".

Yggdrasil

An ash I know that stands, Yggdrasil it's called,
a tall tree, drenched with shining loam,
from there come the dews which fall in the valley,
green, it stands always over Urd's well.
Voluspa. 19.

The World Tree or Yggdrasil is the foundation on which everything in Norse cosmology both literally exists and depends upon to live. *"The tree was immense. It supported, or shaded, high halls and palaces. It was a world unto itself."* Its branches stretch into the far skies above" (Byatt. A.S. 2011. pp.15-16). Its roots go deep into the soil below. Within Its ancient branches are the nine worlds. Under and around its roots are the three wells which provide knowledge, fate and the secrets of creation and destruction.

Odin sacrificed one of his eyes to take a sip from the Well of Mimir Mimir was a giant who was renowned for his great knowledge and wisdom beyond measure. The Well of Urd is where the three Norns live, who weave together the fates of all beings. They water Yggdrasil daily from the well, so it will not perish. Hvergelmir Well is the primordial source of all rivers and at its heart sits a volcanic cauldron deep into Niflheim. Near to this well is the serpent, or Nidhogg, who chews the roots of Yggdrasil in order to make it collapse.

Trees have always been immensely important to the Anglo-Saxon's ancestral Germanic tribes in what is now Scandinavia. If we remind ourselves, according to the Norse myth, even humans are made from two tree trunks. Sacred groves of trees, although associated with Druidic practice in the British and Irish Isles, were found in Germanic tribal areas, described by Tacitus, as consecrated for a specific deity, such as Nerthus. It was usual for a family tree to be close to a house, and the luck of the whole family depended on the survival of this family tree in early Scandinavia and Germany.

The Trundholm Sun Chariot which is in the National Museum of Denmark. This remarkable depiction of the sun being pulled by a horse, dates from 1400 BCE, indicating that is probably older than the Norse mythological story of the creation of the sun.

The Sun and the Moon

The Sun was formed from molten rocks from Muspelheim after the sky was created in order to illuminate the worlds. Sol and her chariot are pursued by a wolf called Skoll, (one who mocks) so moves swiftly across the sky. Mani (the moon) is chased across the night sky by another wolf. called Hati Hrodvitnisson, (one who hates). Eventually Skoll and Hati will catch and consume the sun and moon, and this is the sign of the start of Ragnarök. Interestingly Hati's father is said to be Hrodrsvitnir which is a by-name for Fenrir, the great wolf who will kill Odin at Ragnarök.

Ragnarök

> *Nidhoggr the great worm who gnawed the roots of Yggdrasil came out and sucked the blood from the dead as they lay in the freezing slime. From the Kettlewood where Loki lay bound amongst the geysers...came the loud howl of wolves, wolves in the wood, wolves padding over the snow, wolves with blood on their fangs...*
>
> *Wind time, wolf time, before the world breaks up.*
>
> A.S. Byatt. Ragnarök. 2011. pp.134-5

Next, one wolf will swallow the sun, the other wolf will then swallow the moon and the sky will have no stars. The whole Earth will shake, and Fenrir's bonds will break. The Midgard serpent spews venom into the air and sea. From the fires of Muspelheim comes the giant Surt, a fire giant, whose sword will shine brighter than the sun, The ship Naglfar, made from nails of dead men, will get loose and sail towards the battle steered by Loki, who is free of his bonds.

All the enemies of Asgard will go to the battlefield Vigrid. The Bifrost will shatter under the weight of so many and

Heimdall will sound the Gjallarhorn to warn the Aesir of their approach.

The Einherjar (Odin's chosen warriors who reside in Valhalla) and Aesir are led by Odin to the battlefield. Odin is swallowed by Fenrir but avenged by one of his sons, Vidar, who rips the Wolf's jaw apart, killing him. Thor battles the Midgard serpent, and kills it, only to be overcome by the venom the creature has spat at him. Frey will die because he lacks a good sword, Tyr will kill and be killed by the monstrous wolf Garm. Heimdall and Loki will kill each other and finally the giant Surt will burn the whole earth.

Yet this is not the end, as both the Voluspa and the *Prose Edda* attest to. From this destruction comes re-birth, Baldr returns from Hel, a new Asgard named Idavoll will exist. Two people who hid from the fire of Surt will re-populate the earth, the fields will be green again and the daughter of Sol (the sun) will again brighten the skies.

There may have been some embellishment by Snorri in the *Prose Edda,* to give the tale of Ragnarök some parallels with Christian materials, in particular the two people who populated the world, (in a similar way to Adam and Eve in the Bible) and the burning of the world at doomsday.

Ragnarok is depicted on parts of the Gosforth Cross. The Cross is in the churchyard of St Mary's in Gosforth, and dates from the beginning of the tenth century, when this part of Cumbria was in the kingdom of Northumbria. It was constructed in a similar style to other Viking crosses. The style of the carving is said to depict both Christian and Norse mythology in a similar way to the Jelling Stones of Denmark.

In his 1896 book *The Ancient Crosses of Gosforth and Cumberland,* Charles Parker identified several scenes from Ragnarök on the cross, including Heimdall blowing the horn, Vidar tearing Fenrir's jaws apart, (above) and Loki bound being protected by Sigyn. There is debate as to whether the depiction of Norse mythology on a cross indicates that the Viking rulers still reverenced their old beliefs or were using the symbolism as metaphors for Christian equivalent dogma.

Another theory is that the symbolism in Ragnarök might possibly suggest the seasonal occurrence of death in winter and re-birth in spring. This would be concurrent with seasonal theories and fits with other European belief systems, such as the symbolic battle between Holly and Oak in Druid and neopagan philosophies.

In her 2011 book, *Ragnarök,* A.S. Byatt uses the symbolism of Ragnarök as a metaphor for her experiences as a child in the Second World War. The myths helped her understand the uncertainty surrounding her and gave her a world to escape to when hunger and dislocation became too much. In the world of gaming, several recent creations have shone a light onto the Norse eschatological event; including *God of War Ragnarök* (2022. Santa Monica Studios). This is an action-adventure game for the PlayStation system and the ninth instalment in the series. The story centres around ongoing characters, Kratos, and his son Atreus, who must battle with the Aesir gods, Thor and, primarily, Odin who is determined to prevent his death as foretold at Ragnarök and the protagonists must save the god Tyr who has been imprisoned. We meet many characters, including Angrboda, the *jötunn* and Surt. I am not a gamer, but I have a close family member who takes gaming very seriously, she kindly offered her expertise with a demonstration of *God of War Ragnarök* and pointed me in the direction of a detailed online review which included explanations of the storyline. Although this game doesn't stick dogmatically to the myth, she believes that *God of War Ragnarök* is the most accurate and although convoluted with many twists and turns; this is the game she would recommend to anyone interested in the mythology. To my strictly observant eye, The realism in graphical design is excellent and I enjoyed the story, which I believe is strengthened by its difference from the myths.

The Nornir and the Web of Fate

In Norse mythology, time is intricately woven by the Nornir. These beings are probably goddesses of destiny. The three powerful entities, Urd, Verdandi, and Skuld, are responsible for shaping everyone's destiny – humans, gods, giants and more. They live at the base of Yggdrasil, where every day they feed the tree with water from the Well of Urd, this is also where they spin the threads of fate. The Nornir represent the past, present, and future, and shape the narrative of all existences. Their weaving of fate determines the lifespan, indicating the interwoven balance between the past and future.

The three Norns each have different parts to play in fate. Urd (Fated) is the Norn who represents the past, or things that have already happened. Verdandi (Becoming) is concerned with the present, or what is happening right now, and Skuld (must be) embodies the future or what will happen.

If you wish to work more extensively with the Norns, then I highly recommend Irisanya Moon's book about them: *The Norns, Weavers of Fate and Magick*. Her book is a great introduction to them, filled with ideas and inspiration for building a devotional and ritual practice around the Norns.

Wyrd

This is an Anglo-Saxon or old English word, and is a concept directly linked to fate, it is linked to the Proto-Germanic, *werþan-* meaning 'to come to pass, to become, to be due'. The word can also be connected to the Old Norse *urðror* or Urd, as mentioned above – one of the Nornir and the Well or Urd which feeds Yggdrasil. Related or the same as the Norns and weavers of fate, are the Wyrd Sisters from Shakespeare's *Macbeth* and latterly Terry Pratchett's humorous book of the same name.

Wyrd is woven as you go through life, with the choices you make and their consequences having a direct effect on the weave. So, to some extent Wyrd is changeable with right actions and this can be reflected in the concept of Frith.

Orlog

Orlog is predestined, meaning it is the fate a person is born with – your personal destiny, which is unique to you. The origin of the word derives from Old Norse words similar to "beyond law". The goddess Frigg was said to "know all Orlog" but does not divulge it, (Lokasenna. 29) which suggests that she has knowledge of fate, like the Norns. Indeed, one of her symbols is a distaff, which is used for spinning and weaving.

So far, we have examined the myths, a bit of history and Norse cosmology, which I hope offers a strong context, and a starting point to your own research into these areas of study. As I have said and I will say again, the more information and understanding you have at your fingertips, the better prepared you are to work with deities and spirits; and in turn, your rituals will be enriched and powerful.

Next, we will examine the gods and goddesses in more detail.

Chapter 5

The Gods & Goddesses

The Gods and Goddesses of the Anglo-Saxons

For a scant one hundred and fifty years, after arriving in the post-Roman country of Britannia, the Angles, Saxons, and Jutes were pagan. This, to start with, doesn't give us much evidence of their practices and who they worshipped. That the Anglo-Saxons were illiterate and most of their buildings and therefore, likely also their objects of reverence, were made of wood, gives us further problems. After the Anglo-Saxon's swift conversion to Christianity, during the seventh century, writing and the written word soon followed. By the time Bede wrote his *Ecclesiastical History of the English People* in 731, most Anglo-Saxons preferred to leave out their pagan origins, which, sadly for us, means there is very little written evidence and what there is, has been Christianised. Therefore, we must find alternative methods of exploration.

Firstly, and most obviously, we have the days of the week. All except Saturday are named after an Anglo-Saxon Deity. This gives us a basic framework of the primary gods of the Anglo-Saxons:

Monday – 'Monandæg' – Moon's day, after Mani, the moon god.
Tuesday – 'Tiwesdæg' – Tiw's Day after the god of war and combat Tiw or Tiu.
Wednesday – 'Wodnesdæg' – Woden's Day, after the chief of the Gods, Woden.
Thursday – 'Thunorsdæg' – Thunor's Day, after the god of Thunder, Thunor.

Friday – 'Frigedæg' – Frige's Day after the goddess of home and love, Frige.
Sunday – 'Sunnandæg' – Sunnan's Day after the goddess of the Sun.

The second source of evidence is found in place names and features around England. By far the most commonly found relate to Woden, proving his importance to the Anglo-Saxons. His name is given to the great earth work at Wansdyke (Woden's dyke) in Wiltshire, Wednesfield (Woden's field) in Wolverhampton, and Wembury (Woden's Hill) are all examples of his far-reaching popularity.

Thunor is another commonly found name in the English landscape in places such as Thundersley in Essex (Leah is old English for Wood or clearing in a wood) and Thunderfield in Surrey (Thunor's open land). Thunor was not only the god of thunder, but of weather in general, so would have been significant to the Anglo-Saxon farmer.

Tiw, the Anglo-Saxon god of war and (possibly) justice, features in Tuesley in Surrey, (Tiw's Wood) and Tysoe in Warwickshire, (Tiw's Hill-spur).

The worship of Frige is even more enigmatic and there are very few remnants found in the landscape of England, although it is possible that Freefolk, which was listed as *Frigefolc* in the Doomsday Book is named for her. Also In Hampshire: Frobury, and Froyle which derive from *Freohyll* may mean "The Hill of the Goddess Frige" in Old English.

The third piece of evidence for the existence of Woden is found in the genealogy of nearly all Anglo-Saxon royal lineages. Though does this piece of evidence in fact point to Woden being a man rather than a god? Indeed, there is one striking difference between Anglo-Saxon Woden and the Norse Odin: if we are to believe the later Anglo-Saxon artists, Woden appears to have both his eyes!

So, what does that mean to us? Does it imply that Woden is completely different than the Odin of the Norse pantheon? Could the illustrator(above) have simply made a mistake, considering that the image was created centuries after Anglo-Saxon paganism had been supplanted by Christianity, and the illustrator possibly may not be familiar with the backstory of the God? Or could the two gods be in fact, similar but not identical? Possibly Woden had been downgraded or euphemised from a god to a man. He does, however, still have the prestige to be an ancestor of all Anglo-Saxon royal houses. The above image, which in my opinion, still looks kingly and impressive, could therefore represent a mortal Woden. This is one of those tantalising morsels of the unknown, that will probably remain so.

Written evidence of Anglo-Saxon gods has singular problems. Primarily that they were not contemporarily written, so are not firsthand accounts. Prior to the arrival of the Angles, Saxons and Jutes in Britain, Tacitus's *Germanica* was written around 79 CE. An ethnographic work, describing the Germanic people, (who were likely to be the later Anglo-Saxon's ancestors). Within the book are some clues to the beliefs of the Germanic people along with descriptions of the lands and laws.

One goddess mentioned by Tacitus, stands out because he states that among the seven tribes that worshiped her, one was the Angli who later came to Britain:

> *They are distinguished by a common worship of Nerthus, that is, Mother Earth, and believe that she intervenes in human affairs and rides through their peoples.*
> (Tacitus, *Germanica* Ch.40 Translated by A. R. Birley)

Nerthus an earth goddess, or Mother Earth probably came to Britain with the Angli of the Anglo-Saxons.

Bede in his *Ecclesiastical History of the English People,* published in 731 CE, offers up some tantalising clues to two other goddesses that he believed were known and worshiped in pagan times; the first is **Hrêða.* The only piece of information offered by Bede is that the month of March, or *Hrēþmōnaþ* as it was called in Old English is related to her. Rachel Patterson, in her book *Gods and Goddesses of England* proposes that her name may translate as either glory or victorious. (p.57). This then could hint at a tribal origin and possibly a goddess connected to warfare. We will never know.

The second goddess Bede mentioned who he associated with the month of April, or Eosturmonath in Old English, is Eostre.

Bede even goes so far as to admit that Eostre gives her name to Easter.

The legacy of Anglo-Saxon gods and goddesses, although fleeting in written records, is nevertheless impressive. The city I live in was a Saxon strong-hold and the specific area still has its Anglo-Saxon name which translates as "The Hill on the Shore." Although enigmatic, a bond can be formed with the Anglo-Saxon gods and goddesses – I would recommend doing research in your immediate area, find out as much as you can about its history. If there isn't any written evidence, as this chapter has demonstrated, it doesn't mean they aren't present. All you need to do is sink your hands into the soil and speak to them.

If you are in a country or area that doesn't have a historical link with the Anglo-Saxon's at all, that doesn't mean you can't find and honour them. Heathenry is known for being the faith, (or religion) with homework, and hopefully this chapter has inspired you to find out more. My advice is to read everything, and if you are lucky enough to have Heathen friends, then ask questions.

The gods are there, all you need to do is ask to speak with them.

The Norse Gods and Goddesses

I can be fairly sure that you are at least a little familiar with the Norse Gods. Of the two pantheons I have featured in this book, the Norse Gods are by far, the more famous and well represented gods in today's popular culture. Extremes of information – I have gone from hardly any sources or evidence to work from, to the exact opposite of more than enough and then some! From the highly successful cinematic Marvel Thor, battling against his tricksy "brother" Loki, (who, incidentally, has his own TV series) to the wonderful characterisation by Ian McShane of Mr Wednesday (Odin) in the TV version of American Gods, the Norse gods are everywhere! Indeed, the symbolism of the raven (an Odinic bird) transformed into the three eyed raven summons a young Bran Stark to a mysterious tree and then transforms into an old man, notably missing an eye, in the highly popular HBO series Game of Thrones, is a clear reference to Odin and the World Tree, Yggdrasil. As a pantheon, we are spoilt for choice as there are many books you could pick up.

For those who are totally new to the Norse Patheon then here is a basic overview. The Norse gods are divided up between the Aesir (sky gods) and the Vanir (land gods). Additionally, there are also gods who are *jötunn* or giants. Please be aware that this is an introduction, so I have only written in more detail about some of the key gods and goddesses. If you feel drawn to a particular god or goddess, then as I have said before, this is spirituality with (plenty of) homework!

Odin – The All-Father, one of the three original creator gods.
Frigg – Odin's partner and goddess of the household and marriage.
Thor – The Son of Odin, and God of Thunder.
Baldur – The good and beautiful, Odin and Frigg's son who is killed in an accident.
Hodr – Baldur's half- brother, who is blind.
Heimdall – Son of Odin and the nine waves. He is guardian of the Bifrost, the entrance to Asgard.
Tyr – God of warfare and justice.
Bragi – The god of poetry and eloquence.
Idunn – With the Golden apples.
Sif – Wife of Thor, known for her golden hair and mother of Ullr.
Ullr – A winter God associated with skiing.
Sigyn – Known only as the wife of Loki and the one who catches the poison, stopping it from falling onto her husband.

Njord – The God of the harbour and a Vanir God who was exchanged after the war between the two God races.
Freyja – Daughter of Njord, Goddess of Seidr (Norse magic) love, war and much more.
Fray – Twin brother of Freyja and son of Njord, God of the harvest and peace.
Loki – Oath brother of Odin and known as a trickster God, his origin is mysterious.
Skadi – A Giantess/Goddess associated with winter and married to Njord.
Hel – Daughter of Loki and the Giantess, Angrboda, She is half alive and half dead and rules over the realm of Helheim.
Ran – Goddess of the drowned.
Aegir – A possible god of the sea.

Odin

By far the most recognised and well documented god of the Norse, Odin, is known by many names. Morgan Daimler, in her book on Odin, says he has more than 200, which is not hard to believe considering he is known to wander the earth, or Midgard, when not in council with the other gods. Interestingly, one of his names is *Julfodr*, (Yule Father) and he is not only supposed to be the leader of the Wild Hunt that departs around the winter Solstice to sweep up the souls of the departed, but the original father Christmas figure!

He is, along with his brothers, the creator of the worlds and humans, literally giving us breath and therefore life. He is leader of the gods, and father of many, and married to Frigg.

Odin is the child of the primordial being, Buri, and a giantess, Bestla. He has, famously, only one eye, the other was sacrificed in Mimir's well to gain more wisdom. As a wanderer he is described as wearing a broad grey hat with a brim and wearing a black or blue cloak and carrying his spear, known as *Gungnir*, as a walking stick. Sometimes he has a patch over his missing eye and often with a long grey beard and hair although sometimes he may appear younger.

He is the god of wisdom and poetry, he owns the mead of poetry, aptly named *Odreorir*, (Old Norse meaning "Stirrer of inspiration.") The story of how he obtained this mead, is also a good indication of one aspect of Odin:

> *After the Aesir/Vanir war had ended, the gods on both sides sealed the pact by spitting into a great vat and from this was formed a being called Kvasir. He was the wisest person who ever lived and be became famous for his counsel and advice. He was murdered by two dwarfs called Fjalar (Deceiver) and Galar (Screamer) who brewed mead from his blood. This mead was able to give insurmountable wisdom to anyone who drank it. The two giants got a taste for killing people and took a giant called Gilling out to sea and drowned him for fun.*
>
> *Gilling's son Suttung learned of his father's murder and decided to exact revenge by killing the two dwarfs. The two dwarfs pleaded for their lives and Suttung agreed if they gave him the mead made with Kvasir's blood. He in turn, hid the mead under the mountain of Hnitbjorg and guarded by his daughter Gunnlod.*
>
> *Odin in his endless quest for knowledge decided he wanted to taste the mead so disguised as a farmhand, Odin arrived at the farm of Suttung's brother, Baugi. There were nine servants mowing hay. As he approached them, he offered to sharpen their scythes with a whetstone and afterwards rejoiced at how well their scythes cut the hay. The farm hands decided they wanted to purchase the whetstone, and Odin agreed to sell it, but he warned them, at a high price. Odin threw the stone into the air, and, in their scramble to catch it, the nine killed each other with their scythes. Odin went to Baugi and told him about the*

> *accident but introducing himself as "Bölverkr" ("Worker of Misfortune"). He offered to do all the work of the nine servants on the condition that his reward was. a sip of Suttung's mead.*
>
> *Baugi clearly didn't believe that Bölverkr would be able to do the work of nine men so readily agreed to his payment, thinking nothing would come of it. However, at the end of the growing season, Odin had, of course, fulfilled his promise to the giant, who had to reluctantly accompany him to Suttung to try and obtain some mead. Of course, Suttung refused. The disguised god reminded Baugi of their pact and convinced the giant to help him gain access to Gunnlod's dwelling. This he did by drilling a hole into the dwelling, and promptly changed into a snake to crawl through the hole.*
>
> *He then disguised himself in the form of a charming and attractive young man to beguile Gunnlod as she guarded the mead. He quickly won her favour and secured a promise from her that, if he would sleep with her for three nights, she would grant him three sips of the mead. After the third night, she granted his wish, taking him to the three vats, and consumed the contents of each vat in a single draught.*
>
> *Odin then shape-shifted into an eagle and immediately headed for Asgard. Suttung upon discovering his trickery, also became an eagle and set off in pursuit. Although the giant was hot on his tail, he was unable to catch Odin. The other gods, who were watching, put out containers around the edge of Asgard, which when Odin reached them, he instantly regurgitated the mead. As he did so, though, a few drops from his beak fell to Midgard, (the human world). It is said that these drops are create all bad and mediocre poets and scholars. The true poets and scholars, however, are those to whom Odin dispenses his mead personally.*

As you can see from this story, Odin has the power to shape-shift, can be deceptive and ruthless in his pursuits.

The All-Father, (another of his names) is also associated with battle frenzy, or certainly inspiring it. The first part of His name, *Odh* means frenzy. You may come across this in more detail when studying the Norse myths and sagas relating to the infamous Berserkers who are ruthless fighters, supposedly feeling no pain. A good example of this in modern popular culture is shown in the film, *The Northman,* The film is based around the legendary story of Amleth, who becomes a Berserker when he flees after the death of his father.

Odin's home is called Valhalla, where the chosen fallen warriors feast and drink mead after fighting all day. It is believed to be every warrior's deepest wish to be an Einherjar and get to Valhalla to feast with Odin at the high table.

His knowledge of magic is twofold, he is the master of Runelore and Runic power and he is a practitioner of Seidr magic which he learned from the goddess Freya.

His creatures are two ravens, Hugin and Muninn (Thought and Memory) who fly through the worlds and bring him news. He has two wolves, Geri and Freki and rides and eight-legged horse, Sleipnir.

Thor

There's probably not much you don't know about this immensely popular god. If you ask anyone to name a god in the Norse pantheon, he will probably either be the first or second name mentioned. His fame has been pretty consistent and continues to the present day with Marvel comics and the hugely successful string of 21st century movies. These movies, although not especially accurate to the myths, (which is a bone of contention to purists) portray Thor in a heroic light as defender of the human race and bring him to new generations of young admirers, as well as older Marvel comic fans. Chris Hemsworth, who played Him, is now considered the face of Thor in the 21st century. Continuing this trend, Thor is also portrayed as a schoolboy in the recent Norwegian Netflix series, Ragnarök, (2020) In the series, Magne (David Stakston) accidently discovers he is really the thunder god and must fight against the destruction of his town.

Thor is historically described as having a bristling red beard, whilst this is contended by Snorri Sturluson who described him as having hair fairer than gold, which fits with his modern portrayals in film.

He was a beloved and highly important god of the Norse people, this can be attested by the description of Uppsala, (Now Gamla Uppsala in present day Sweden) a huge temple complex, and possible centre of religious practice during the Viking period. Chronicler Adam of Bremen made an account of the temple in the eleventh century in his work *"Gesta Hammaburgenis Ecclesae Pontificum"* in which he states that "the people worship three gods, of which the mightiest Thor sits in the middle of a triple throne."

Thor's father is Odin and his mother is Jord, possibly a giantess or the Earth. He is married to Sif with the golden hair and has he has two children, Modhi and Magni by a giantess, Jarnsaxa, and a daughter called Thrud (or Trud) with Sif.

One of the most famous and widely known symbols of both Thor and Heathenry in general, is Thor's hammer, Mjolnir. Thousands of Mjolnir pendants have been found in the Scandinavian countries, Britain, Germany, and Russia from archaeological excavations, indicating the popularity of Thor. Mjolnir was crafted by dwarves as gifts for the gods, and Thor used it to kill many giants and is one of the Aesir's main weapons against them. Conversely, Mjolnir was also used to bless marriages and fertility of the happy couple. This leads me to one of my favourite stories about Mjolnir and Thor: The Lay of Thrym. The original can be found in the *Poetic Edda*:

Thor awoke one day to find his hammer, Mjolnir was missing. This was an absolute catastrophe for the gods – without the gods best weapon, Asgard would be totally vulnerable to the giants attacks.

Thor, who was hot-headed, flew Into a rage, and began searching high and low, but Mjolnir was nowhere to be found. Thor asked Loki, the trickster for help in finding it.

Freya, the goddess owned a beautiful cloak of falcon feathers, which could shape-shift you into a falcon upon wearing it. She lent it to Thor and Loki so that they could find the precious hammer. Loki, who knew how to shift his shape, donned the cloak, and flew far searching for word of the hammer. He had surmised that it had probably been stolen by the giants, so he rode the winds to their homeland, Jotunheim.

Thrym, chief of the giants admitted gleefully that he had stolen it, it was buried eight miles below the ground. He would return the hammer on condition that Freya became his bride.

Upon Loki's return to Asgard, be broke the news of the hammer and Thrym's bargain. Everyone was furious but especially Freya. Odin called a counsel to discuss their options, and Heimdall suggested that Thor travel to Jotunheim disguised as a bride, and the giants being so stupid, would not recognise Thor and he could claim back his hammer plus take his vengeance on them. Thor was unsure, but Loki pointed out, that if he didn't go along with Heimdall's idea, Asgard would be destroyed by the giants and all the gods would be slain.

Thor's bridal outfit was the finest and all the goddesses' brought things for him to wear, along with an extremely opaque veil! Freya even leant him her precious necklace Brisingamen. Loki offered to go with him as his lady-in- waiting and easily shape-shifted into the character.

Thor's goat-drawn chariot swept away into the sky and the finally arrived at Thrym's hall. Before the pair entered, Loki

> *advised Thor to not speak and let him do all the talking. (Thor had a very gruff voice!)*
>
> *As Thor and Loki entered the hall, Thrym's giant sister accosted the pair and tried to look under the veil. She was suspicious of Freya-Thor's reluctance to remove it. However, Loki smooth-talked her, saying that the "bride" was saving herself just for Thrym., Further suspicions arose when Thor singlehandedly ate an entire ox, eight salmon, and all of the dainties that had been prepared for all the women – not to mention many barrels of mead! Thrym eyed Freya-Thor suspiciously, and he declared that he had never in his whole life seen a woman with such an appetite. Loki quickly devised a response: "she has not eaten for eight days and eight nights," he claimed, "due to wedding nerves." Thrym seemed to accept this. He was overcome by a desire to kiss his bride. When, against Loki's protestations, he peeled back the veil, Thor's eyes glared at him so intently that they seemed to burn holes right through him. He exclaimed, "Never have I seen a maiden with piercing eyes!" Loki smoothly explained that while Freya been unable to sleep, so fierce was her desire for her marriage.*
>
> *Then began the ceremony, it was customary for the hammer to sanctify their union. When Mjolnir was laid in Thor's lap, he grabbed its handle and slew first Thrym, then all of the guests. The pair returned to Asgard.*

I believe this story shows both the power of Thor and his humorous side. After all, it could be argued that if the god didn't want stories that make him look anything other than the perfect icon, this story would not exist. Though it raises the important subject of gender and transgender in Norse mythology. Loki is known to switch sexes and shape shift to suit the needs of various quests, including this one. I posit that gender to the gods is not defined in such rigid terms as male and female.

Interestingly Thor is often portrayed as a slightly loutish muscle man who loves a fight and enjoys a drink (or twenty). Yet In the *Poetic Edda,* Thor wins a battle of wits with Alvis (The "All-Wise") a dwarf who claims he is going to wed Thor's daughter, Thrud. Thor matches him in a skaldic riddles contest until day breaks and Alis is turned to stone.

Thor's other possessions include a chariot pulled by a pair of goats called Tanngniost (Tooth Gnasher) and Tanngrisnir (Snarl Tooth) who are eaten every night and, providing their bones are all preserved along with their skin, will magically be as new each morning and his hall is called Bilskirnir, which has five hundred and forty living spaces. His magical belt doubles his power.

Frigg

Frigg is a goddess of immense importance in the Norse pantheon. Although sometimes she seems to be overlooked and simply classified as the wife of Odin, the All-Father. Her presence in the Eddas is often lacking, however I believe this is simply because the Eddas have been cleansed to suit a Christian audience and written by men, usually of the cloth (i.e. Priests, monks or similar). Therefore, I strongly believe we need to re-think and consider Frigg to be of huge significance to the Heathens who worshipped her. Indeed, this can plainly be attested to by the fact that Venus was called "Frigg's Star" in old Norse and Orion's Belt was known as "Frigg's Spindle." This to my mind, proclaimed a deep devotion by the people of the Nordic countries.

Her roles within the Norse pantheon seem clear; firstly, as the wife of Odin, the All-Father, and Ryan McClain in his book, *Frigg: Beloved Queen of Asgard* posits that She is, therefore, The All-Mother. She is the goddess of marriage, motherhood including childbirth, and the mother, or mother figure for the Aesir. She is most famously, the tragic mother of Baldr.

At the start of this tale, Baldr is plagued by terrible dreams of misfortunes and disasters befalling himself. Odin his father, using one of his many disguises, goes to Hel's realm to consult a dead seeress who could look into the future. To Odin's dismay, she confirms that Helheim is making read for Baldr's arrival and that Baldr will die soon, although she is vague about how it will happen. With a heavy heart, Odin returns to Asgard and tells the grief-stricken gods all that he has learned. Frigg is beside herself and decides to take a journey through the nine realms to speak to everyone – all entities in the cosmos from stones to mountains and obtain an oath that they will not harm Baldr, her beloved son. The journey takes many months, the travelling is arduous, but Frigg will do everything in Her power to protect her son.

After all the millions of oaths have been given, she believes she has prevented his death. The gods have a party and make a sport of throwing everything they could find at the Golden God for fun. The partying lasts many days.

However, Loki, the trickster goes to Frigg in the disguise of one of her handmaids to double check with her if indeed everything has sworn an oath to leave Baldr unharmed. Frigg is fooled by Loki's disguise and confides in him that all beings have, all except mistletoe, which she considered too small and spindly to bother with.

With a glint in his eye, Loki departs and finding some mistletoe growing on a mighty oak in the forest, he makes a simple dart from one of the many stems. Returning to Asgard, he finds Höðr, the blind god who is Baldr's brother. Hodr is seated outside the entertainment and Loki – the master of persuasion and trickery – encourages him to join in with a special gift of a dart he even helps him aim…

All the gods are mortified at the death of Baldr, Frigg is inconsolable, and Odin completely numb. All that can be heard in Asgard and throughout all the realms is wailing and sobbing as the worlds turn to darkness. Frigg in her grief asked if any god would be brave enough to venture into Helheim to ask Hel to return Baldr to the gods. Any ransom would be offered, although Frigg knew that Hel was Loki's daughter and might not accept. Hermod, Odin's son, stepped forward. Odin gave him Sleipnir, and he rode for nine nights and days to reach Helheim. When he finally approached the hall, he found Baldr seated at the high seat to the side of Hel, an honoured guest eating and drinking with the dead.

Hermod begged Hel to release Baldr back to his family. He beseeched her that all things wept and grieved for their beloved golden god. Hel eventually said she would give back Baldr if all things in the nine realms, dead or alive, did weep for him. She tasked Hermod to ask everything and when she was satisfied, she would allow him back. As Hermod made to leave, Baldr gave him Draupnir, Odin's ring that had been burned upon Baldr's pyre with his body, as proof that he had been to Helheim.

Upon his return to the Aesir, Hermod relayed the deal and gave Odin his ring, then set out to travel everywhere to witness the grief of the worlds. After many months of travelling and securing the word of every being that they did indeed weep for Baldr, he neared Asgard. Hermod stopped at a cave to rest and take sustenance. His heart was light as he was sure that Baldr would be back in his rightful place soon. He was started to hear a noise and found an elderly giantess behind him. He almost casually asked her if she wept for Baldr, sure that he knew her answer. His heart grew cold though as she announced that he had no love for Baldr and was glad he had died.

Baldr would remain in Hel's halls forever.

Loki would face revenge.

That's another story.

Frigg is portrayed not only as the grieving, loving mother, but also as resourceful with a knowledge of all things and the ability to speak the language of beings and plants. She is devoted and patient in this story. Her grief is one which would speak to all grieving parents and her favour would have probably been sought on the child-birthing bed. Other aspects Frigg is connected with are the household and spinning.

The parentage of Frigg is somewhat mysterious, although her father is said to be Fjorgyn of whom we know nothing. Her hall is known as Fensalir which means home in the marshes, and could, therefore, associate her with wading birds, such as the heron. She is known to have a falcon cloak, similar to Freya, and her cart is said to be pulled by rams.

Baldr

I have told the story of Baldr and his death in relation to his mother Frigg above. He is married to Nanna, and they have a son called Forseti. There is little mention of his wife and child in the Eddas except in the story of his death. Baldr's home is called Breidablik, which, Morgan Daimler suggests means "the far shining one". Snorri goes on to place Baldr's home in heaven! I believe this is Snorri's Christianity linking Baldr with Christ in his purity.

Freya

Freya or Freyja is probably the most popular goddess of the Norse pantheon. She is one of the Vanir, who were likely originally nature-based deities. Although, she is considered to be one of the Aesir by Snorri Sturluson. and indeed, he says that she is "along with Frigg, the most notable..." (*Prose Edda*. p.42).

Freya's family includes her brother, Frey, sometimes considered her twin. Her father is Njord the harbour god and her mother unknown. Freya is married to the mysterious Od and they have a daughter called Hnoss.

Within the mythologies it sometimes appears as though Freya's inclusion is merely as the object of lust for giants or magical people, as evidenced in the story of Thrym (see under Thor). In the tale of the mysterious smith who makes a deal with the gods to build a wall around Asgard, Freya is one of the three prizes demanded for building the apparently impossible wall in record time. Personally, I find it rather uncomfortable in various re-tellings, that Freya's adamant dismissal of the smith's demands is largely ignored by the gods of the Aesir. However, it is Loki, not Freya, who is made to recompense and restore balance when the smith seems to be very close to doing his impossible task. Her reputation is called into question in several tales; notably in Lokasenna, Loki declares she has been lover to everyone including elves, but then again Loki accuses all the goddesses of indiscretions in this story.

One of the most renowned stories involving the goddess is how she acquired the necklace of Brisingamen. The story explains that Freya saw the necklace being made by four dwarves, Álfrigg, Dvalinn, Berlingr and Grérr, who were extremely skilled craftsmen. She offered them gold and silver, but they would only part with the necklace if the Goddess would spend a night with each of them. Freya agreed and received the necklace in return. Although the story could be considered controversial, Morgan Daimler posits that this tale shows that Freya has agency and is willing to sacrifice to gain what she wanted, in a similar way to Odin gaining the wisdom of the Runes, and I agree with them. Freya has control over her own sexuality and power.

Cats are strongly connected to Freya, and she is said to ride a chariot pulled by them.

Freya is known to be the goddess of Seidr magic. It is said in the *Ynglinga Saga* that she taught Seidr to the Aesir, and Odin is known as a prominent practitioner of Seidr.

It is said that Freya may claim half the battle dead, (before Odin) who come to reside in her hall, Sessrumnir, (which means many seats) and is situated in Folkvangir. This, to me, implies that Freya could be also a battle and death goddess.

Frey

Frey is Freya's brother and one of the Vanir gods who was exchanged after the Aesir-Vanir war, along with Freya and his father Njord. He was one of the three gods honoured at the temple of Uppsala according to Adam of Bremen, which affirms his importance to the people. He is considered to be the founder of the Yngling Royal house of Sweden, where he was manifested as Yngvi. Indeed, the name Frey means "Lord" in Old Norse, which is not a personal name.

The most famous story involving Frey is his infatuation with the giantess Gerd. On glimpsing her beauty, he became lovesick, sending his manservant Skirnir to woo her. This doesn't start well and finally Gerd agrees to the match after Skirnir threatens her with a Runic curse. They are married nine nights later.

Frey was given the realm of Alfheim by the gods after cutting his first tooth, which is where he supposedly lives. He owns two precious objects, the ship Skidblandnir, and the boar Gullinborsti. These were two gifts presented by the Dwarves after Loki stole Sif's hair.

At Ragnarök, Frey will fight Surt the giant without his sword and will die.

Loki

> *Give a dog a bad name they say, and never was there any dog with a name worse than mine. I am a bad person I expect. You will begin with your suspicions about me and I don't expect to convince you otherwise.*
>
> (Melvin Burgess. *Loki*. 2022. p.3)

Loki is to put it mildly, a controversial character in Norse mythology. He is both a force for chaos and consternation for the Aesir, a trickster with a vital role to play in the end of times, Ragnarök, yet he is also Odin's oath brother and the founder of pivotal treasures, such as Mjolnir and Gungnir. His offspring include Odin's eight-legged horse Sleipnir, and with the giantess Angrboda, Hel, the guardian of Helheim and protector of the dead, Fenrir the wolf who will swallow Odin at Ragnarök, and Jormungand the world serpent whose venom kills Thor at Ragnarök.

His wife is the Aesir goddess Sigyn who is so devoted to him that when he is bound and forsaken by all the other gods, she sits patiently with a cup and collects and prevents the poison from landing on him.

Loki has become extremely prominent in popular culture, largely thanks to Marvel and their depiction of Loki in the Thor films. The Marvel Loki is slippery – sometimes he's on Thor and the good guy's side, and sometimes he's on the side of the enemy, mainly though, he is on this own side. The Marvel character has proven so popular that he even has his own TV show. Louie Stowell has produced a hugely popular series of books for children about Loki, in which he is transformed into an eleven-year-old boy and placed on earth by Odin as punishment with Heimdall as his father and "a terrifying giant called Hyrrokkin" as his mother. In these humous books, Loki goes through many of the issues faced by teenagers today, with the added animosity of his god-ness or rather lack of it. In Melvin Burgess's 2022 novel, *Loki* the god is brought to the present day and offers his own unique interpretation of the Norse myths and sagas including his eye-witness account of Odin hanging from Yggdrasil. In *American Gods*, by Neil Gaiman, the protagonist, Shadow Moon, is befriended and supported in jail at the beginning of the book by a character called Low Key Lyesmith, who turns out to be non-other than Loki himself.

Loki Stone

Recently I had the opportunity to visit Kirkby Stephen Parish Church in Cumbria to view the famous Loki Stone. The stone which dates from 900-1000 CE is the remains of a shaft from a heavily carved cross, almost certainly Viking in origin, and similar to many from Northumbria and the Isle of Mann. This important piece of Viking archaeology was found in the nineteenth century by accident when the chancel was being rebuilt. Originally the figure was thought to be a bound devil, but later speculation grew that it was Loki bound after being caught by the other gods before Ragnarök. The theory that Loki has possibly been amalgamated into the Christian devil has been further endorsed by Dagulf Loptson in his book, *Loki* (p.11). The Kirkby Stephen Church seem to agree with this assumption, pointing out the apparent horns by the figures head as evidence of the Devil. Personally, given that the cross is clearly Scandinavian styled, very similar to the nearby Gosforth Cross, and other examples in Sweden, I believe this is Loki. The horns? Well possibly they might be merely the style of carving or maybe even Loki's hair? As the very top of the figure's head is missing, we do not know for sure in this respect.

Another controversial subject I would like to examine here is the possibility that Lodur, mentioned in the *Poetic Edda* as one of the three gods who gave life to the tree trunks, Ask and Embla is in fact, Loki by another name. Loki is Odin's oath brother, which could suggest that he was there at the beginning of the world. However, in Snorri's *Prose Edda,* he names two entirely different gods as the progenitor of the first humans, Ve and Villi. (p.18). So, although many have theorised, there is no clear answer to this, and I leave you to make up your own mind on this subject.

Loki is a controversial god, and some Heathens will not include him in their rituals at all, whilst others accept him for what he is. Of course, it's up to you to decide whether to engage with him, I will point out that Dagulf Loptson includes a warning in his book, pointing out that Loki is a trickster and unpredictable. He posits wisely that bringing Loki into your life will bring transformation and probably chaos. So, you have been warned.

Heimdall

Son of Odin and the nine waves of the sea. Interestingly in old Norse folklore the waves of the sea are called sheep and the last, or tenth is a ram. In old Norse the word for ram is *heimdali.* He guards Asgard and protects the entrance, the Bifrost Bridge, from his hall called Himinbjorg. He is sometimes considered an ancestor of humans as he consistently went among people and fathered children with them. He is also the most reliably generous to humans, meaning he is the god to ask for assistance in matters of household disputes and diplomacy.

His horse is called Gulltopp, which means golden forelock. He is known for owning the Gjallarhorn, which is so loud it can be heard anywhere in the nine realms. The Gjallarhorn will signal the start of Ragnarök. (Daimler. 2022. p73).

If you want to connect to Heimdall, visit the coast and visualise the god riding the surf as the waves come in. Of course, if you see a rainbow at any time, give thanks to him.

Tyr

Tyr, is a warrior god who also dispenses justice, and was considered the god of the Thing, an Iceland where justice and laws were discussed. If you visit Iceland today, you can still visit the Thingvellir which is now an archaeological site.

The most famous story about Tyr involves the giant wolf Fenrir, one of Loki's children. The gods raised him from a pup after he was brought before Odin along with his siblings. Only Tyr was brave enough to feed the wolf, but because of the prophecy and the rate at which Fenrir was growing, the gods decided to bind him. Ordinary chains and ropes did nothing, so the gods turned to magic and asked the dwarves to make them a magical shackle. The rope was so fine and thin that Fenrir was suspicious and stipulated that one of the gods must place their hand in his mouth whilst he was bound with the rope. The only god brave enough to do this was, of course, Tyr. Inevitably the magical rope held Fenrir so tightly that he could not move, and Tyr lost his hand.

Tyr will battle another bound hound at Ragnarök, this time a wolf called Garm. The prophecy states that they will kill each other.

In their book *Pantheon: The Norse,* Morgan Daimler theorises that Tyr may be a far older sky god, who was later replaced by

Odin (p.85). This would explain his apparent lack of appearances in much of the mythology.

Hel

Daughter of Loki and the giantess Angrboda and sister to Fenrir the wolf and Jormungand, the world serpent. Hel is the goddess who rules over most of the dead. She is famously considered half alive and half dead, or half white and half black – which could mean she is half rotting, with a possibility of blood pooling after death making her dead side darken in a grotesque manner. She was given the domain of the dead by Odin after she and her brothers were seized by the gods. Interestingly, Hel resides in Helheim not Niflheim, although she may have been put there at the beginning and it is likely that the two worlds are very closely related.

In the Eddas her most noted role is in the tale of the death of Baldr, as he is taken to Frigg's hall to reside until Ragnarök. Any amount of pleading by the gods in various ways, does not bring him back to them. Let's pause there and consider for a moment, although Eljudnir (Hel's hall) is in Helheim, a cold and dark realm, this is the place most of us will end up at after we die. Baldr and his wife Nanna, who threw herself on the funeral pyre after her husband's death, are given a place of honour at Hel's table. I don't believe Baldr suffers, but he is respected, and honoured with feasting. Though Baldr is biding his time, he is entertained and shown privilege by his host. Are we sure that He and Nanna aren't happy here?

Although the *Prose Edda* suggests that Odin threw Hel down to Niflheim, He then gives her rule over the dead of nine worlds – those who have died from old age and natural causes (ie not in battle). The only other beings who have rule or sway over the dead, are Himself, Freya and Ran. I would suggest that this is not a punishment but a mark of esteem.

Hel is an important deity in modern Heathenry, for example, in 2024 the annual UK Asatru summer moot was held in her honour with a wooden Godpost created especially. Some Heathens honour Hel at Samhain, which is a festival of the dead, and many ancestors are honoured, so it seems only right to honour their guardian.

Chapter 6
The Vaettir

The Vaettir are the spirits that inhabit places such as buildings, like your house, the land, including your garden, the local park or a wild place, for example. Vaettir means spirits in Old Norse and here I am using the term to collectively talk about all the spirits that are not gods or mythological creatures. Another name for the Vaettir could be the *Genus Loci* in Latin. Perhaps in your corner of the world, your local nature beings might be known as fairies, elves or brownies. The Vaettir are the beings you might have a direct, or maybe an even closer relationship to, than, say the gods, because their actions can have a more immediate impact on your life and spiritual practice.

Folkloric evidence suggests that the industrial revolution, plus societal changes in belief, account for tales of landvaettir (land spirits) lessening and/or not being taken seriously. In other countries, such as Ireland, belief in sprits, and other-than-human beings is still strong – famously the Tuatha de Danann, (the supernatural race that inhabited Ireland before Christianity) were supposedly driven underground by the victorious Milesians and forced to dwell only in the otherworld. Access to the Tuatha is though portals and liminal places such as ancient monuments in the landscape. Fairy trees – Rowan and Hawthorn trees often standing alone in a field are sacred to the fairy folk, (or Sidhe in Ireland) they may also be a gateway to the fairy world. These trees are treated with the utmost respect so as not to offend the Sidhe. Similarly, in Scandinavian folklore, the *Nisse,* or *Tomte* (the house spirit, usually associated with farmsteads) can cause havoc and mayhem including damage to the property or livestock if they have been offended. In Iceland belief in the *Huldrufolk* – or *Hidden People* – is still current.

Certain holidays – *New Years Eve, Thirteenth Night,* (January 6th, or *Twelfth Night* as it is known in other places), *Midsummer Night* and *Christmas Night* are significantly linked to the Huldrufolk. On *Midsummer Night,* for example, special bonfires are lit for them and if you happen to be sitting at a crossroad, an elf may try to seduce you!!

When I first moved into my current residence, in fact, even before I moved into the house, I had a strong feeling, when visiting, that my family and I were welcome. Within a month of moving in, my House Wight introduced Himself to me. He told me that is what He is, and that's what I should call Him. He is very protective of the house and gets upset if He feels we are neglecting certain jobs, such as cleaning the guttering or washing the windows. He appreciates food/ drink offerings which I leave in a certain place that I have designated His sacred space. If I forget to make the offerings at the regular agreed time, small things start happening – like my jam won't set, or my cake doesn't rise properly, or bits of my jewellery disappear – until this is rectified. I often chat to Him, or tell Him things, and although it's not a two-way conversation, I have a strong sense that He is listening. Importantly, He protects the house when I am away, or not home and if I am alone in the house and someone knocks the door, I am confident that he has taken a good long look before I even answer. This becomes very apparent if he is wary, and on one occasion he even apparated to stop me answering the door!

I believe I am lucky that my House Wight is present, and that He has a keen sense of responsibility to the house and us as its residents. Long before my house was here, the area was a forested valley and it is my supposition that he has been here for a very long time, perhaps migrating from the forest or coming with earlier settlers. Historically, Vaettir or similar inhabitants of dwellings and buildings were commonly found in the countryside, or places not overpopulated and with a certain amount of wild nature.

In modern times, it may seem hard to believe that Vaettir or Wights, could be ever present in our multi-storey high-rise dwellings, and with the busyness and pace of our lives, their presence could easily be missed. I would suggest that you spend some time in silent contemplation or meditation to reach out to them. You could try making an offering in an area of your dwelling that is relatively undisturbed, something homemade, or a drink, maybe bread or butter.

If you are fortunate enough to have a garden, then contacting the Landvaettir – land spirits might be possible. Spend time outside, meditating, paying attention to the plants, earth and trees, or simply connecting with the ground by going barefoot. Sink your hands into soil, plant things, grow flowers. I have found the best time to connect with these Landvaettir is at night when my neighbourhood is relatively quiet. Be present, and conscious of everything around you and listen. Find words that have meaning and speak them, to the land with heart and intention. Leave offerings in a secluded spot – a simple flower arrangement, clean water, and anything not poisonous to creatures who inhabit the space – interestingly, I have found eggs are a particular favourite! Every year I also walk the bounds of my garden, scattering water and offering words of protection. This is my contract with the Landvaettir who dwell in my garden, I will protect and care for the area within, and in return they will protect it from outside influences, unless invited in, of course.

After you have established a relationship, you might find their presence particularly strong near certain plants, or at certain times of the year or month – mine are very present at full moon, and this is usually when I make fresh offerings on my little tree-stump altar.

Landvaettir – land spirits – in other less cultivated places, like sacred sites, and wilder places are prevalent in countries such as Iceland. There are famous stories of rocks or boulders inhabited by Wights or other Vaettir, that happen to be right in the path of the construction of roads, meaning the whole project is diverted to protect the spirit. There are similar stories from Ireland where a fairy tree, is present and therefore houses or road locations have to be re-thought. The lesson here is that respect for the other-than-human beings is of the utmost importance.

Here is a fine example of the perils of upsetting the Landvaettir: A friend of mine once made the mistake of taking some hawthorn clippings and flowers from a local nature reserve without asking permission from the Landvaettir – in this instance, The Good People, on May eve, (Beltane) and was plagued by very bad luck. I, having a strong relationship with them, made offerings and contacted them through journeying to ask what this person could do. I was told in no uncertain terms that the person had to offer a piece of precious silver, (a piece of jewellery in this case) and apologise by making offerings of bread, milk and honey on Samhain, Imbolc, Beltane and Lammas, every year. Immediately this was done, their bad luck began to lift and good luck prevailed.

In 2023 I walked part of the most northerly established pilgrimage, St Olav's, which has a network of routes all over Norway and Sweden. We chose to walk part of the 84km path from Singsås to Trondheim which is through forests and visits St Olavkippen. This very remote area has extremely powerful Vaettir – the site itself was said to be originally a place of pagan worship. Stories say there was a fierce fight between the force of Christianity, Olav Haroldsson, and the so-called mythic creatures such as trolls, dwarves and goblins, (Landvaettir). The resulting battle was so intense that the rock was spilt in half. Some of the Landvaettir had transformed into strange fish creatures and to counter this, Olav created a deep cavern in the mountain which he filled with holy water, which became a holy well. The water was said to be magically powerful, and from that day forth, when farmers visited the pastures nearby in the summer, they would come and fetch the holy water in closed buckets, and this was splashed over the pastures in a ritualistic act. If the summer had been good, the farmers would make an offering or sacrifice in the well. For example, a metal objects were thrown into the source while reading a prayer. Today it is marked by a tree cross.

The area surrounding this legendary story is very still, as though holding its breath and there is a strange sense of having dozens of eyes following you. When we visited, at the beginning of summer, it was rather damp and chilly with a slight drizzle. The rocks had the look of an ancient hewn tapestry, covered in pock marks, and worn away through millennia of harsh winters to a pale grey. The crack in the rock itself is shocking, and I could easily imagine the cracking sound of Olav striking his staff into the very heart of the landscape.

I lay on the stone nearby and listened. Words, however intuitive, were not necessary, the Vaettir here were unused to many travellers, and were at once curious, although tentative. I closed my eyes and let my mind drift into swirling dreams of an ice laden ash tree with fiery leaf-tips. A blast of sunshine stirred me and when I opened one speculative eye, I was sure I saw something retreat into the treeline. I had a strong sense that Vaettir vastly outnumbered us. As we gathered our things, I found a small, indented hole to the side of the rock and left an offering of teeny tiny shell from my local shoreline.

Chapter 7

The Ancestors

Most people will be familiar with honouring ancestors – this could be simply visiting a graveside on the anniversary of the person's death, laying flowers and spending time remembering them. In some cultures, around the world, the ancestors have a specific festival; when everyone goes to their places of rest, and has picnics, with the deceased as the honoured guest. Evidence of ancestor veneration exists in any country you find a burial mound, tomb or similar.

In Heathenry, the ancestors you will probably have the most contact with are your Disir. The Disir are your female ancestors who protect their ancestral line, (i.e. you). In some rituals it is usual to honour the Disir at the beginning of the rite in order to be protected during the ritual itself. In October, around the time of Halloween, is a celebration known as the Dísirblót. Offerings of drink or food, and often words, such as poems are given. It is a time to honour female relatives and thank them for their continued protection. At this time of year, the end of summer, towards Midwinter it is common to set up an ancestor altar, with pictures of your dead loved ones, with candles and appropriate gifts of food or drink.

You may want to spend time discovering more of your family tree, and learning about your personal ancestors, this can be done by visiting older relatives and asking questions, or using online websites designed for specifically for this. You may be able to find official documents, such as past years census and birth certificates, via government websites. Family doesn't need to be biological, as we all know, and it might be worth spending time researching the people whom you consider your family, whether these are close friends or your adopted family, for example.

Of course, looking into family history can be problematic emotionally. There may be issues of historical trauma and abuse, which make this task very challenging. I found it a huge stumbling block many years ago, when studying Druidry and ultimately it meant that I could not move on with Druidry because of painful and disturbing truths that were uncovered. After this I found Heathenry – a faith without the expected requirement of examining your family history and gods accept you as you are. Through Heathenry I side-stepped the inherited trauma, and instead, with meditation, journeying and guidance, now dedicate myself to becoming a worthy ancestor for my family, one who they are proud to remember and call their kin – though I doubt if they'll write a family Saga about me!

Ancestors are likewise honoured in Heathen gatherings, called Symbels. This is similar to a Blót in that offerings of drinks and words are made, usually with a communal drinking vessel, like a horn or similar, and this is then passed from person to person. There are usually three rounds of toasts, firstly to the gods, then individual ancestors or friends who have died. Sometimes people offer a poem or story in the third round, or they might boast about their achievements.

More details about this and adaptations for solitary Heathens in the next chapter.

Chapter 8

Devotion, Ritual & Celebration

Prayer

Hail to the Day! Hail to the sons of Day!
Hail to the night and her kin!
With gracious eyes may you look upon us (two),
And give victory to those sitting here!

Hail to the Aesir! Hail to the goddesses!
Hail to the might fecund earth!
May you give eloquence and native wit to this glorious pair
And healing hands while we live!
Sigrdrifa's Prayer in the *Poetic Edda*

In Heathenry, as in most religious practices around the world, it is common to offer prayers. A prayer is the simplest form of devotion, and I am guessing that you probably have an idea of how they go. These could be to a specific deity, or all the gods, for example. The prayer above is made by the Valkyrie Sigrdrifa after she is awakened from an enchanted sleep by Sigurd, so he can ask her advice. This prayer is from the *Poetic Edda, Lay of Sigrdrifa* stanzas two and three. A prayer can be given in silence or aloud, the most important aspect is that it is sincere and comes from the heart. It is a great way of connecting and communicating with a god or gods and offering thanks. Prayers can be part of a formal gathering or done in private, even in meditation. I find the best place to offer a prayer is beside my altar or in a ritual space that I have created and usually I light a candle and sometimes offer mead. It's really up to you how formal or informal you wish to be.

When I first came to Heathenry, or even before, I found the idea of praying difficult. When I was a child, I was forced to subjugate myself and pray to a god who was not only judgemental but aloof. It was done through fear – of my family's wrath if I didn't do it, and the god's mollification for any supposed sins I had committed. There was no love or devotion involved. However, I now wanted to show my devotion, my love and my gratitude to the Heathen Gods, so I learned through journeying and meditation, how to pray, how to honour and how to offer gratitude. I have found that the act of creating a prayer, and saying it with deep meaning, is a fulfilling act of devotion. I never imaged it would open a line of communication that is rewarding, and I feel blessed by it.

Writing a Prayer and Kennings

A self-created prayer doesn't have to be a complicated affair. A simple thanks, as long as its heartfelt is enough. Another way to honour the Gods in prayer is through kennings. This means you are describing the God, using figurative language instead of their name, such as, by one of their actions or something they are known for. For example, Odin could be called a World Wanderer, or a Spear Shaker. It is an excellent device for helping you to really consider every aspect of a God, and because it was traditional in Old Norse and Icelandic to use kennings in poetry, you are fostering a deeper relationship with the God. Here is a simple example of a prayer I wrote to Odin featuring kennings:

Hail Odin
Breath Giver, World Wanderer, Runic Master, Battle Lover, Sage Seeker.
I thank you for your continued guidance and favour.
I request that you grant me clear mindedness and inspiration in my writing.

Please accept this mead as my humble offering.
Odreir's keeper, I honour you always.

Altars

I have three altars and one more that comes out once a year; one for the Gods, which is in a quiet room away from the general traffic of my house, a place I can be alone, to pray, meditate, light a candle, and spend time with the Gods, or simply spend a few moments in peace. I have Godposts on my altar, a cup for mead, or water, a bowl for other offerings, Runes, and other seasonal items. I change my altar cloth depending on the season, for example, in the summer I have a golden cloth for the sun, at midwinter and Yule, I have a silver cloth for moonlight, frost, and snow. My second altar is outside and primarily used in the summer as an offering place for the Gods and Landvaettir. It is made of a wooden tree stump, quite simple and here I offer flowers, drink, sometimes food and prayers. My third is for my House Wight, and it is in an inaccessible place in my kitchen, I offer milk or dairy, homemade bread and either flowers or other home-made food items or produce I have grown. I offer here as instructed by my House Wight, roughly four times a year with an extra one at Yule. I give thanks to Him and request He continues to protect my property. My annual Altar is for my ancestors, it is not a permanent one. On it I have photos of my blessed blood ancestors, candles and a representation of the Goddess Hel, the altar cloth is dark purple. This altar is only present around Summers End or Winterfyllith.

An altar can be as simple or complicated as you feel necessary, and all altars are different. I have found that placing an altar in a slightly out of the way place means it is not disturbed and offers some sanctuary. Some of my Heathen friends have very visible altars on their mantlepieces or in their main living areas, others don't feel the need for an altar or at least a permanent one at all, and this is all perfectly fine. You are free to honour the Gods / Vaettir / Ancestors in any way that is right for you.

One of the most important components of my primary altar is a small Godpost, a carved representation of a god, which in keeping with written tradition is a centre piece for my devotions. It that was carved for me by Chris who is a solitary Heathen living in the south of the UK. I was intrigued to hear about his Heathen practice and how this is reflected in his creations.

When did you discover Heathenry? What pulled you to it as a spiritual practice?

> *I was raised with gods, monsters and mythology from an early age, my mum bought me books on Greek myth and legend and the stories of King Arthur. I'd say I really discovered my spiritual path in my late teens. I'd always felt different when surrounded by nature – in the depths of the forest or staring at the vastness and beauty of the sea, I believe as humans it's something that's imprinted in our genetic heritage. In my teens I started to question where I came from – not just in a familial sense but the stories of the people who inhabited the land where I was born. Back then there was no internet (imagine that!) I found the rich cultures and fascinating histories of the Celts, the Saxons and the Vikings and I started to see how their gods and their stories related to the natural world. The more I read the more it resonated with me and that feeling I had when immersed in nature, it all just fell into place and I knew that what I felt was what people have always felt – all over the world ancient cultures have sky fathers, earth mothers, gods of love, war and death and that their characteristics and stories helped our ancestors to contemplate and comprehend their place in the world.*

How do you personally practice your Heathenry?

I tend to be quite solitary in my practice, most of what I do takes place within me just sitting quietly with my gods with a fire and an offering of food, drink, flowers or something I have created. No grand gestures that are visible to the eye, no costume or spoken words – it's a very personal thing, there is no right or wrong way, everyone must find their own way to commune with the gods and this is mine. I base my ritual observations primarily on the cycles of the sun, the solstice and equinox celebrations often at home in my own sacred space devoted to the gods but I love to visit sacred places too, those that are well known and those that you must find for yourself and feel their sacred energy.

When did you start making Godposts and why?

I created my first Godpost – a little Thor from a scrap of pine back in 2013. Prior to that I had always drawn and painted and over the years the characters I was drawing started to take on this blocky, chiseled kind of appearance and I had the curiosity of wondering what one would look like as a physical 3D presence. One day whilst mundanely clearing out our garden shed the last thing left in there on the floor in the far corner was this little offcut of pine timber. I saw it l, I picked it up and I knew this was the piece. I went to work with a knife and a basic set of micro chisels, I wanted to create a god whose identity was unmistakable and so it had to be Thor with his hammer! I worked on him over the course of a few days and found it to be really immersive, relaxing and enjoyable. He turned out pretty well and I posted a few pictures on my social media because I was pretty proud of him and straight away a few friends asked if I could make them something similar. Then a few of their friends, and a few of their friends – and so Gungnir Godposts was born! It's incredible to think how it started and how big a part of my life and my identity it has become – all from that scrap of timber on the floor of my garden shed!

How do you incorporate your crafting into your Heathenry?

The two really go hand in hand. In creating the presence of a god, I really delve into who they are, I contemplate the stories associated with them from their perspective, their traits and characteristics, what they symbolise and what they would have meant to our ancestors

To you, what does a Godpost represent?

Oh, I could talk about this forever! For me a Godpost is the crystallisation of contemplation – the giving of physical form to that which is divine within nature, within the cosmos and within human nature. It is a sacred and soulful expression shared with our early ancestors across time.

What words of advice would you offer a new Heathen?

I'm truly excited for anyone finding their way to this spiritual path. It offers more than you could possibly imagine. The only advice I give to anyone is to read the stories of the gods. Get to known their traits and characteristics the way you know your own friends and family. Feel how they relate to your own experiences and to the natural world. Find your own way to relate to them and to express that relationship.

Rituals

As this book is an introduction to Heathenry, I am going to give a basic outline of two rituals: Blóts and Symbels, along with some historical context. These two rituals are the cornerstone of most Heathen practice, and although the two examples are group orientated, they can easily be amended for an individual. I have used the group example to give a foundation on the rituals, but they can be changed or used in any way that you see fit. These outlines can be used simply as a reference or a starting point for creating your own rituals. The most important point to remember is the intention. Even though the two I have outlined are aimed at groups, I have included some information afterwards on how to make them accessible for individual practitioners.

Blót

Blót is an Old Norse word that means 'Sacrifice'. In the time of the Vikings and probably the Anglo-Saxons, this would have required the killing of an animal, almost certainly livestock. The Stentoften Runestone discovered in Blekinge, Sweden and dated from the seventh century, describes a blót of nine male goats and nine stallions, to bring about the fertility of the land. After the animal(s) was/were sacrificed, it/they would be cooked and consumed in a feast. In modern times, the sacrifice has been translated into an offering of drink and a few words. I have attended communal blóts which feature two of three rounds of toasting, with everyone in a circle around a central fire and followed by a potluck meal shared with everyone – noting that food was put aside from the feast, in honour of the god or whoever the blót was in honour of. During Covid times, I attended online blóts, where everybody brought their own drink and toasted together.

A Traditional Blót – You Will Need:

Beverage (Mead is most common)
A Vessel (A drinking horn is usual)
A Bowl for collecting the poured libations

- All Participants face inward in a circle. (Around a fire, an altar or candle.)
- The beverage is poured into the vessel while invoking the god or whoever the blót is for.
- The vessel is raised with a toast to the god or being.
- The vessel is passed from person to person, and each offer a toast to the god or being and take a sip or kiss the horn, for example.
- When the vessel gets back to the first person, they give a libation into the bowl.
- Continue around the circle with toasts to other people, heroes etc.
- When the rounds of toasting have finished, the vessel is laid down and the gods or beings are thanked for their presence.

In modern blóts it is usual to create sacred space with fire and water, this is done by nominated people who will walk around the circle three times. After this, there is usually a period of energy raising which is done with drumming or dancing. After the blót has finished, it is customary to have a meal together, and socialise.

Symbel

The word Symbel is Old English and means feast or banquet. Symbels or Symbel-like feasting is mentioned in *Beowulf* and other Anglo-Saxon poems such as *Judith*. In the *Poetic Edda, Lokasenna* stanza eight – *"A place to sit and feast..."* usually, this feasting takes place in a great hall around a long table with horns of mead and many tales of heroic deeds. Oaths and obligations were given, and bonds are built. In contemporary Heathenry a Symbel focuses on sanctifying oaths and similarly to a blót, toasts can be given to the gods, as well as remembering the ancestors. It is traditional to sit at a Symbel and customary for them to take place indoors. Interestingly, these days a feast is not common, although Symbol means this.

Symbel – You Will Need:

Beverage, (Mead, beer or non-alcoholic drink)
A Vessel, (Usually a drinking horn)
A Bowl for libations

- All participants are seated.
- The beverage is poured into the vessel and blessed.
- The vessel is passed around from person to person, and a toast is given to a god or goddess.
- When the vessel returns to the beginning, a libation is poured into the bowl, and the vessel is refilled if necessary.
- The second round everyone toasts to ancestors, a person who is no longer alive, or a hero.
- Again, when the vessel returns to the beginning, a libation is poured into the offering bowl and vessel re-filled.
- The third and any subsequent rounds are open, and for boasting of deeds or telling a story, or making an oath. It is typical to offer thanks to the host, or organiser in these rounds.
- Rounds may continue or the Symbel is formally closed, depending on the group.

For the Individual – The Blót and Symbel are easy to adapt for a single participant. Follow the first steps until you come to pass the offering vessel around the circle of other people, simply skip this and go to the second toast and then any aspects relating to group activities. Instead of having a meal with the community, I would suggest having a meal with a God/dess. Have a place at the table for the God/dess and serve food to them. Or entirely skip the meal. With the drumming etc, perhaps replace with a piece of pre-recorded music that you like, and dance to it? Remember the Gods, Vaettir and ancestors (obviously depending on who you have invoked) are listening, so don't be afraid to speak your truth.

Boasting (Old English gilp)

For many reserved people, (me included) this may seem a daunting task, and it is perfectly acceptable in a Symbel to simply make a toast instead. However, I can assure you that it gets easier with time and practice. The boasts don't have to be huge heroic deeds or magnanimous gestures, they can be as simple as "I finished all my coursework today," or "I managed to do ten thousand steps every day this week." Sometimes people tell a story of a humorous event that happen to them, and this is a great way to break the ice and build community relationships.

Oaths (Old English bēot)

While boasts can be light-hearted, an oath given in a Symbel is taken seriously, primarily because you have many witnesses including the gods or beings invoked. This may require some preparation beforehand, and your words should be chosen with care. If nothing else, an empty oath, or an oath that you have no intention of fulfilling will make you appear foolish. Obviously sometimes life doesn't go to plan and things may change, and this is perfectly fine, an oath can be modified, and your kin will be understanding in this situation. The best policy in this situation is to speak honestly and from the heart.

Celebration

In Western society there are traditional celebration days with holidays attached, such as Christmas and Easter, based on Christian dogma. Other religions have different festival days, for example, Diwali, which is a Hindu festival although observed by Sikhs as well, and these are incorporated into the yearly calendar. In Heathenry there no officially endorsed holidays, simply because there are many different factions under its umbrella. There is also little historical evidence for specific pre-Christian holidays, and therefore most festival days are essential reconstructions of approximations based on the scant references in texts such as the sagas and Eddas. Many are a combination of this, along with living traditions in the Northern lands, mixed with elements of folklore. Here I am going to draw from these pots of information and share the most commonly recognised observance days.

Yule

This is probably a familiar term to most of you, and is often associated with the Christian Christmas, mainly because they are very close together in the calendar. Usually celebrated from the winter solstice, Yule is a very important holiday in the Heathen calendar. Odin is said to lead the Wild Hunt at this time, and in the Anglo-Saxon calendar, *Mōdraniht* (Old English meaning Mother's Night) was held on what-is-now Christmas Eve, celebrating both female ancestors, and goddesses, especially Frigg. Today in Sweden, on the lead up to Yule/Christmas, it is common to find the shops full of marzipan pigs, this is a direct connection with the old Norse tradition of *heitstrenging*. This event took place on Yule evening and involved swearing solemn oaths about future actions to be taken in the following year, sometimes with a hand on the bristles of the sacrificial boar which would be eaten at the Yule festivities. In Scandinavian countries to this day, pork is the traditional Christmas meal.

Dísablót

Usually held in February although the exact date is not definite, this celebration is to honour the Disir – female protective ancestors and sprits, along with venerating the Norns and Valkyries. This coincides with the Swedish festival of Disting, which originally combined both a market at Uppsala, a *Thing* (a huge meeting which included the common people and the governing bodies) and a blot, which according to the *Yngalinga Saga,* was presided over by the king of Sweden in honour of the Disir. To modern Heathens, Dísablóts tend to be family affairs which celebrate the female line and our protective spirits.

Walpurgisnacht

Although now named after a catholic saint, Walpurgisnacht was originally called *Thrimilci,* which is the Anglo-Saxon name for what is now the month of May. A month of plenty – 'in that month the cattle could be milked three times a day' according to Bede. Walpurgisnacht, as it became is celebrated on the 30th April, which is the same as the Celtic holiday of Beltane. It is associated with witches and other dangerous creatures who gather to feat and make merry. The holiday is also linked with fertility – of the land and humans, and therefore in modern Heathenry has a connection with both Frey and Freya. It is a time to honour relationships of all kinds including romantic. Offerings are sometimes made to the Vaettir to ensure good luck.

Midsummer

The summer solstice is the time to celebrate midsummer, with food, dancing maypoles and flowers in your hair! Second only to Yule in importance in the Heathen calendar, with various rituals for health and prosperity for the next half a year would be made, bonfires would be lit, and feasts would be had. In northern Scandinavia, this is the time of the midnight sun, when it never really grows dark. It is a time to celebrate the light and warmth of the season, for soon darkness will return.

Winterfyllith

Winter Nights, called *Winterfyllith* which is Anglo-Saxon for the month of October and means 'winter' s full moon.' It marked the official start of winter. Today the festival is largely reconstructed, and its theme of remembrance and honouring the dead, is similar to other pagan and Christian rites marked at this time of year, such as Samhain and All Hallows Eve. Feast and stories are told of the honoured dead, with rituals and offering made. I focus my altar on the goddess Hel, who is guardian of the dead, and their protector in Helheim. Furthermore, I create a temporary altar to my ancestors of blood and bond. Here I remember people of significance who have passed to Hel's care over the past year and my own relatives. I give honour to my Disir.

Chapter 9

The Runes

I know I hung on a windswept tree
Nine long nights,
Wounded with a spear, dedicated to Odin,
Myself to myself,
On that tree of which no man knows
From where its roots run.

With no bread did they refresh me nor a drink from a horn,
Downwards I peered;
I took up the runes, screaming I took them,
Then I fell back from there.
(*Hávamál*, – Sayings of the High One. 138-139. *Poetic Edda*)

Odin, in the *Hávamál,* hung from the mighty Yggdrasil, after being wounded by Himself with a spear – sacrificing Himself to Himself – and only after nine days and nights did he gain Runic knowledge. Does this seem like a high price to pay for a simple writing system? It could be argued that writing is the foundation of all wisdom, communication and understanding. Odin is the insatiable wisdom seeker and unafraid to surrender Himself for knowledge, after all, He gave his eye for a draught of water from Mimir, the great sage's well to gain just a sample of the immeasurable wisdom it contained. So, what do these words mean to a Rune seeker? Simply that to gain knowledge you must be prepared to commit yourself, that the journey will be hard, difficult and often challenging. That only when you have given everything will you find wisdom and enlightenment. This may seem like harsh words to the modern audience, but if you wish to establish a strong, arcane and deeply meaningful relationship with the Runes, then you need to work at it.

My own Heathenry is heavily Rune focused. I began my journey with the Runes when I was a teenager many years ago. From the first glimpse – on the cover of Prediction magazine in my local newsagent, I was impulsively drawn to their energy, and they have been my life-guides ever since. When I barely existed, when my life was filled with transience and anguish, the Runes were an anchor, I crafted them, read copious books about them and found a solace in them that is profound and impermeable.

> *The Runes you must find and meaningful letters...*
> (*Hávamál*, – Sayings of the High One. 142. The *Poetic Edda*)

If you are not very familiar with the Runes, then I suggest doing a quick internet search for them, and I guarantee you will find hundreds of wonderful, inspiring and excellent resources about them. These articles usually relate to the most commonly known: the 24 Runes of Elder Fuþark system. This is the oldest known Runic alphabet and dates roughly between the 2nd and 8th century CE. However, there are at two other Fuþark systems that are of equal importance to understanding both how our Heathen ancestors perceived their world and how their writing changed and developed over time. The Anglo-Saxon Runes was the writing system used from the 5th century onward until roughly the 11th century CE in Britian and related areas. The Anglo-Saxon Futhorc consists of between 26 and 33 Runes and was developed directly from the Elder Fuþark. It was the predominant alphabet used by the Anglo-Saxons during the migration period, which began to be replaced by the Latin alphabet after Christianisation.

The Younger Fuþark, sometimes known as the Norwegian or Danish Runes, essentially replaced the Elder Fuþark from the

9th century in Scandinavia; it is a simplified system of writing, with only 16 Runes, and was the main alphabet during the Viking Age.

Evidence of the use of Runes is found throughout Britain, the Germanic countries, Scandinavia and much further afield, including as mentioned previously, in the great Hagia Sophia mosque of Istanbul. Runestones offer some of the finest examples of the use of Runic writing, notably, the famous Jelling Stones in Denmark. Runestones are very often commemorative – the oldest of the Jelling stones was raised in memorial by King Gorm, for his wife Thyra. The two massive stones are associated with the formation of Denmark as a country and are part of the UNESCO world heritage site. Many Runestones have carvings and pictures, often from mythology, which express the deep reverence of the people who carved them. Objects found in archaeological digs sometimes include Runic inscriptions, these often stating the owner's name. I believe this intimate personalisation only adds to the intrinsic value and brings the object to life in a pertinent and tactile way.

> *...do you know how to question, do you know how to ask...*
> (*Hávamál,* – Sayings of the High One. 144. The Poetic Edda)

Working with the Runes within your own Heathenry is a potent devotional practice, and one that not only enhances your relationships with the gods but is a direct connection with the history of our ancestors of faith. For a complete guide to using the Runes for divination, I would recommend Kylie Holmes' *Pagan Portals: Runes* which is readily available. In her introduction, Kylie says "*From my own experience, the Rune Stone meanings are there for you to tap into your own intuition; you can let the Runes teach you what they are about...*" (p.1) which I would agree with. Runes are very intuitive and the more you work with them, the greater your understanding of the message they want to impart to you will be.

The Elder Fuþark is the most popular Runic system, and widely available. It is likely that if you purchase a set of Runes, these will be the ones you will get. There are many resources available which detail the meaning of each rune and recommendations for divination use. The twenty-four Elder Fuþark Runes are present in the Anglo-Saxon Futhorc, with similar, if not the same meanings, hence I have created a table with the symbol in both Anglo-Saxon and Elder Fuþark, approximate pronunciation, the corresponding letter and which includes the relevant section from the Anglo-Saxon Rune Poem. I have used the Rune poems because they are an excellent primary text to illuminate the denotation of each individual Rune and further, the different systems they came from. The three notable poems are the Anglo-Saxon, the Norwegian and the Icelandic. The latter two relate directly to the Younger Fuþark, with the former giving the meaning to both the Elder and Anglo-Saxon Futhorc

ANGLO-SAXON & ELDER			
ᚠ	Feoh Fehu	f	**WEALTH** Wealth is a comfort to all men; yet must every man bestow it freely, if he wishes to gain honour in the sight of the Lord.
ᚢ	Ur Uruz	u (oo as in phew)	**AUROCH (PRIMAL)** The aurochs is proud and has great horns; a great ranger of the moors, it is a creature of mettle. it is a very savage beast and fights with its horns;

ᚦ	Þorn Thuraz	th	**THORN** The thorn is exceedingly sharp, an evil thing for any knight to touch, uncommonly severe on all who sit among them.
ᚫ	Os Ansuz	o	**GOD (WODEN)** The mouth is the source of all language, a pillar of wisdom and a comfort to wise men, a blessing and a joy to every knight.
ᚱ	Rad Raido	r	**RIDING (JOURNEY)** Riding seems easy to every warrior while he is indoors and very courageous to him who traverses the high-roads on the back of a stout horse.
ᚳ	Cen Kenaz	k	**TORCH** The torch is known to every living man by its pale, bright flame; it always burns where princes sit within.
ᚷ	Gyfu Gebo	g	**GIFT** Generosity brings credit and honour, which support one's dignity; it furnishes help and subsistence to all broken men who are devoid of aught else.
ᚹ	Wynn Wunjo	w	**BLISS** Bliss he enjoys who knows not suffering, sorrow nor anxiety, and has prosperity and happiness and a good enough house.

Continued

ᚻ	Haegl Hagalaz	h	**HAIL** Hail is the whitest of grain; and is tossed about by gusts of wind it is whirled from the vault of heaven and then it melts into water.
ᚾ	Nyd Nauthiz	n	**NEED** Trouble is oppressive to the heart; yet often it proves a source of help and salvation to the children of men, to everyone who heeds it betimes.
ᛁ	Is Isa	i	**ICE** Ice is very cold and immeasurably slippery; it glistens as clear as glass and most like to gems; it is a floor wrought by the frost, fair to look upon.
ᛄ ᛃ	Ger Jera	j (y)	**HARVEST** Summer is a joy to men, when God, the holy King of Heaven, suffers the earth to bring forth shining fruits for rich and poor alike.
ᛇ	Eoh Eihwaz	Poss Y	**YEW** The yew is a tree with rough bark, a guardian of flame and a joy upon an estate. hard and fast in the earth, supported by its roots,
ᛈ	Peorð Perthco	p	**JOY** Peorth is a source of recreation and amusement to the great, where warriors sit blithely together in the banqueting-hall.

ᛉ	Ilx Algiz	x	The Eolh-sedge is mostly to be found in a marsh; it grows in the water and makes a ghastly wound, covering with blood every warrior who touches it.
ᛋ	Sigel Sowelo	s	**SUN** The sun is ever a joy in the hopes of seafarers when they journey away over the fishes' bath, until the courser of the deep bears them to land.
↑	Tir Tiwaz	t	**Glory (Tiw the God)** Tiw is a guiding star; well does it keep faith with princes; it is ever on its course over the mists of night and never fails.
ᛒ	Beorc Berkana	b	**BIRCH** The poplar bears no fruit; yet without seed it brings forth suckers, its lofty crown which reaches to the skies. Splendid are its branches and gloriously adorned for it is generated from its leaves.
ᛖ	Eh Ehwaz	e (ay)	**HORSE** The horse is a joy to princes in the presence of warriors. A steed in the pride of its hoofs, when rich men on horseback bandy words about it; and it is ever a source of comfort to the restless.
ᛗ	Mann Mannaz	m	**MANKIND** The joyous man is dear to his kinsmen; since the Lord by his decree will commit the vile carrion to the earth. yet every man is doomed to fail his fellow.

Continued

ᛚ	Lagu Laguz	l	**SEA (WATER)** The ocean seems interminable to men, if they venture on the rolling bark and the waves of the sea terrify them and the courser of the deep heed not its bridle.
ᛝ ᛜ	Ing Ingwaz	ng	**ING (The God)** Ing was first seen by men among the East-Danes, till, followed by his chariot, he departed eastwards over the waves. So, the Heardingas named the hero.
ᛟ	Éþel Othella	oe (Ø as in German ur)	**ESTATE or ANCESTRAL LAND** An estate is very dear to every man, if he can enjoy there in his house whatever is right and proper in constant prosperity.
ᛞ	Daeg Dagaz	d	**DAY** Day, the glorious light of the Creator, is sent by the Lord; it is beloved of men, a source of hope and happiness to rich and poor, and of service to all.
ᚨ	ac	a (ah)	**OAK** The oak fattens the flesh of pigs for the children of men. Often it traverses the gannet's bath, and the ocean proves whether the oak keeps faith in honourable fashion.

ᚫ	aesc	ae (aih - air without r)	**ASH** The ash is exceedingly high and precious to men. though attacked by many a man. With its sturdy trunk it offers a stubborn resistance.
ᚣ	Yr	Y (eu)	**A BOW** Yr is a source of joy and honour to every prince and knight; it looks well on a horse and is a reliable equipment for a journey.
*	iar		**POSS EEL OR SERPENT** Iar is a river fish and yet it always feeds on land; it has a fair abode encompassed by water, where it lives in happiness.
ᛠ	ear	ea (ae plus a = aih-ay) or ee	**POSS A GRAVE OR EARTH** The grave is horrible to every knight, when the corpse quickly begins to cool and is laid in the bosom of the dark earth. Prosperity declines, happiness passes away and covenants are broken.

As you can probably surmise, the Anglo-Saxon Rune Poem has been written down towards the end of Runic usage, roughly the 9th century CE, when the country was largely Christian. There is speculation that it was either copied from an earlier, now lost text, or originally from an oral tradition. The meanings of individual Runic symbols used by the Anglo-Saxons are very visual, for example, ᛋ which is the Sun Rune, and consequently the connotation of the sun is brightness, joy and hope as specified in the corresponding Rune Poem., it can also suggest focus and illumination depending on the enquirer's question.

Several of the Anglo-Saxon Runes are linked with the Gods – ᚩ is Woden's Rune, ᛏ Tiw's Rune and ᛝ is Ing's (or Fray in Norse Belief) Rune. Trees in addition, feature prominently in this Rune system, which denotes their importance to the Anglo-Saxons. The accompanying words from the poem, "The oak fattens the flesh of pigs for the children of men…" in relation to the ᚪ Oak Rune is directly linked to the age-old practice of the common of the mast during pannage – pigs were turned out in the early autumn to feast on the fallen acorns and offers a unique perspective on Anglo-Saxon customs and the daily life of the people. Some of the Runes have rather obscure meanings, and this symbology offers a glimpse into the Anglo-Saxon psyche – what was important, what held shared significance to the people at the time. A good example of this is the * Rune that represents either an Eel or serpent, both of which probably have very different connotations today.

Below is my table of the Younger Fuþark with both Norwegian and Icelandic Rune Poems:

YOUNGER FUTHARK			Norwegian Rune Poem	Icelandic rune poem
ᚠ	fe	f/v	**Wealth** Wealth is a source of discord among kinsmen; the wolf lives in the forest.	Source of discord among kinsmen and fire of the sea and path of the serpent.
ᚢ	ur	ooo, u, ø	**Iron** Dross comes from bad iron; the reindeer often races over the frozen snow.	**Rain** Lamentation of the clouds and ruin of the hay-harvest and abomination of the shepherd.

ᚦ	thurs	th/dh	**Giants/ jötunn** Giant causes anguish to women; misfortune makes few men cheerful.	Torture of women and cliff-dweller and husband of a giantess.
ᚬ	as	a, o, ae (aih – air without	**God/Odin** Estuary is the way of most journeys; but a scabbard is of swords.	**Odin** Aged Gautr and prince of Ásgardr and lord of Valhalla.
ᚱ	reidh	r	**Riding/Journey** Riding is said to be the worst thing for horses; Reginn forged the finest sword.	Joy of the horsemen and speedy journey and toil of the steed.
ᚴ	kaun	k, g	**Ulcer** Ulcer is fatal to children; death makes a corpse pale.	Disease fatal to children and painful spot and abode of mortification.
ᚼ	hagall	h	**Hail** Hail is the coldest of grain; Christ created the world of old.	Cold grain and shower of sleet and sickness of serpents.
ᚾ	naudh r	n	**Need** Constraint gives scant choice; a naked man is chilled by the frost.	Grief of the bond-maid and state of oppression and toilsome work.
ᛁ	isa/iss	ee, i	**Ice** Ice we call the broad bridge; the blind man must be led.	Bark of rivers and roof of the wave and destruction of the doomed

Continued

ᛅ	ar (plenty)	aah. A	**Plenty** Plenty is a boon to men; I say that Frodi was generous.	Boon to men and good summer and thriving crops.
ᛦ	yr (yew)	ee	**Yew** Yew is the greenest of trees in winter; it is wont to crackle when it burns.	Bent bow and brittle iron and giant of the arrow.
ᛋ	sol	s	**Sun** Sun is the light of the world; I bow to the divine decree.	Shield of the clouds and shining ray and destroyer of ice.
↑	Tyr		**Tyr** Tyr is a one-handed god; often has the smith to blow.	God with one hand and leavings of the wolf and prince of temples.
ᛒ	bjork		**Birch** Birch has the greenest leaves of any shrub; Loki was fortunate in his deceit.	Leafy twig and little tree and fresh young shrub.
ᛘ	madhr	m	**Mankind** Man is an augmentation of the dust; great is the claw of the hawk.	Delight of man and augmentation of the earth and adorner of ships.
ᛚ	logr (sea)	l	**Water/Sea** A waterfall is a River which falls from a mountain-side; but ornaments are of gold.	Eddying stream and broad geysir and land of the fish.

"....do you know how to interpret..."
(Hávamál, – Sayings of the High One *144. The Poetic Edda)*

The simplest routine I have is one which is easy to start your Runic path with. First thing in the morning, after you have made your tea, and in a moment of quiet, before you are disturbed or must rush around, clear your mind, and focus it on asking the Runes for guidance for the coming day. Then as you are thinking this, draw one Rune out of their bag. You will probably naturally be drawn to one as you move your hand around the bag. Study the Rune closely, try to imprint it in your mind. Find out what this Rune represents and use this as your focus over the day. It may simply tell you that the day will be good, or it may offer a deeper meaning. As your experience grows, your ability to intuit the Runic meaning will be.

An excellent way to get to know the Runes is to mediate with each one. I spent a week with each Rune focusing only on that Rune, I mediated daily, drew it, drew what it symbolised to me and wrote about it in a journal I made especially to do this. As you deepen your relationship with the Runes, you will automatically become able to intuit their meanings without referring to a book.

Below is an example mediation that you can use or adapt as you wish.

Firstly, find a place you feel most comfortable to sit or lie for a time, and one that will not be disturbed. If you find lighting a candle or incense or playing music helps you to relax, then do so.

Before you start the meditation, have in mind the Rune you wish to focus on, (I have chosen Feoh, ᚠ *for this meditation, simply because it is the first Rune). Hold this Rune in your hand, face up so its energy can flow to you. Run your finger along the shape of the Rune.*

Sit or lie in your preferred position and take a deep breath, allow your exhalation to be slow and measured, feel any tension leave your body as you breath. Concentrate on this feeling of relaxation and repeat the breathing as you feel necessary.

Once your mind is still, imagine yourself surrounded by a golden protective light, this gradually encloses your body starting at your feet, up your legs, through your core, into your hands and fingers. It gently climbs your neck and over your face until it encloses your completely.

You become aware that you are gently floating in darkness, in the silent void of Ginnungagap, the place before time and space. Allow the quiet emptiness to surround you and enjoy being free of your body and all things.

Gradually you begin to see a tiny spark from Muspelheim, the distant land of fire, floating towards you. At the same time a droplet of ice is moving towards you from the opposite direction. This is from the land of Niflheim, the distant land of ice. These two tiny pieces get closer and closer, and as they do, you reach out your hands and take both bringing them together.

As these two elements come together, you are transported to a golden place, you become aware of your surroundings, and see that you are in a room full of golden coins that shine brightly. You are dazzled by their brightness and without thinking, fill your pockets with them. You go to the door; you see lush fields filled with livestock. The whole area is abundant and the sun shines brightly down on this beautiful place. You draw in a deep breath of the sweet rich smell of the land. It seems like paradise as you walk along the path, admiring everything around you.

At the end of the path, you notice the beautiful area has started to change, the land looks worn, and becomes barren, trees disappear, and as you look closely there are no animals at all. This is a wasteland, and everything is barren. You decide to turn back to the lush farmland, but as you turn, a small very thin boy is standing before you, with his hands out and eyes filled with despair. Instantly you reach into your pocket and give the child your coins and at this moment, you see that it was not money you put into your pocket, but grains of wheat that can be ground down to make flour or sown to grow crops. On receiving the wheat, the child instantly transforms into Frey who smiles at you and scatters the grains far and wide.

You watch with wonder as the land becomes abundant, filled with animals, trees and verdant pastures. After He has finished, Frey places in your hand a single amber stone, on which the Feoh Rune is carved. You thank the god for His gift and walk back up the path towards the doorway into the building.

As you pass through you find yourself in the welcoming darkness of Ginnungagap again and enjoy a moment of relaxation before beginning to return to your physical body,

Gently, you feel your toes and legs, move your fingers, and shoulders. When you are ready, open your eyes, and return completely to the physical world. Stretch yourself and have something to drink and eat to ground yourself.

As you work more with the Runes, you may find the meaning will shift into one that is unique to you personally – the Runes are shrewd and emotive allies, making them powerful tools to understanding your destiny. If you haven't already, now is the time to create your own book of Rune meanings, or Runic journal; fill it with anything related to them – readings and drawings, meditation records, your feelings, etc.

> *Do you know how to carve...do you know how to colour...do you know how to sacrifice...*
> (*Hávamál*, – Sayings of the High One. 144. The *Poetic Edda*)

Crafting your own Runes is the next and most important step in your relationship with them. The problem with buying Runes from another person is twofold; firstly, the crafter's energy with be held within their nucleus, and although the crafter may have cleaned them before you received them, there may still be residual feelings attached to them. Secondly, crafting individual Runes yourself is a power exchange between you and its meaning, making the act of creation a sacred one. In the *Hávamál*, – Sayings of the High One, it states that:

...the mighty sage coloured
And the huge Powers made
the Runemaster of the gods carved out.
(142. The Poetic Edda)

Odin, the Runemaster, carved, empowered and coloured Runes. Really there is no higher example to follow than that.

I have crafted many sets of Runes myself, even before I read the *Hávamál* or the Eddas. The first set I crafted when I was a teenager, I used sea washed stones from my local beach, and painted each Runic Sigel with acrylic paint. These Runes served me well into my adulthood, however I found that the gradually wore down and chipped off. This set I still have, but as I went through life, and my spirituality changed and grew, this set's energies only seemed to speak of the past, of my youth and not the present.

A few years ago, I had the wonderful opportunity to visit the Orkney Islands, decided to craft a new set from stones collected at various beaches on the coast, places I connected with spiritually on my journey around the islands. Before I began picking the stones, I centred myself and sitting on the beach, placed my hands into the sands, the sea and stones. I stilled myself, slowed my breathing and listened, my hands communicating physically with the land. In this way, I asked the land, and the Landvaettir if I may take some pebbles, and what they would be used for. If I had felt they didn't want me to do this, I would not have taken any. Luckily for me, I was given permission from them.

After I returned home, I placed the stones on my altar, and there they stayed until it was the right time to carve them. I then created a sacred space, mediated with each stone to discover which Runic sigil would merge suitably with each stone's energies and marked them with a pencil accordingly. I then carved them with a Drimel (a mini drill that will mark stone) whilst using galdr – chanting the individual names over them. They were then replaced on my altar.

I created this ritual of dedication for my Runes.

Ritual to hallow, empower and dedicate Runes to Odin:
This ritual can be done inside or outside but be aware that it may get a bit smoky so make sure the place you hold it has ventilation.

For this ritual, you will need:

A candle or fire
Incense
Sacred or blessed water in a bowl
A representation of Odin (i.e. a Godpost or statue)
Some earth on a plate
Suitable music or a drum to raise energy
Mead and a cup or horn, plus a bowl to hold libations

Optional:
A copy of the *Hávamál* in English (you can print one from the internet)

Begin by walking the edges of the circle whilst beating your drum, or with music simply walk it, seven times.
Follow this by walking around again with either the fire or incense, and then with the water, gently flicking it.

Return to the centre and closing your eyes, call to your Disir asking for their protection in your ritual.

Acknowledge and honour the Vaettir, (*you can call them in if you so wish, depending on your relationship with them*).

Hail Odin, Runemaster and carver of Runes, I request your presence at my ritual so I may dedicate my Runes to you and gain intimate knowledge of their power. (or words of your choosing).

Recite extracts from the *Hávamál*, from stanza 138 onwards as much as you like.

These Runes I have carved and now hallow with fire, *(pass each through the flame being careful not to burn yourself, and chanting each Rune's name).*

I hallow with water, (*drop into the water, or splash with water. Chanting each Rune*).

I hallow with air (*pass through incense smoke, chanting each name*).

And earth (*place each in the earth and leave them there. Chanting each name*).

**Optional: Odin, Runemaster, as you sacrificed yourself to gain the knowledge and power of the Runes, I offer my blood in honour of this sacrifice. (using a needle or a sharp implement, make a nick in your finger and smear blood onto the Runes).*

Odin these Runes I dedicate to you and ask that you imbue them with your energy so they may guide and challenge me, but always be true.

Pour mead into the cup and raise it.

Hail Odin

Pour some of the mead into the offering bowl, then take a sip.

Odin, I thank you for your presence at this ritual of Runic consecration. Hail and farewell.

Thank any other beings you have asked to be preset at your ritual.

My honoured circle of Disir, I thank you for your continued protection and wish you well.

Blow out the candle, and then walk the opposite way around the circle you cast to clear its sacred state.

*I chose to use my own blood as a symbolic sacrifice, in honour of Odin's sacrifice to gain the Runes. It adds another, deeper layer of your own energy mixed with the Runic energies. It is a powerful way to charge them and additionally, makes them specifically your own. Other Heathens I know, have used their menstrual blood, which adds an intrinsically personal charge to your new Runes. This is, of course, a completely optional part of the ritual, and one which can easily be left out.

I must add here that using bought Runes at the start of your journey with them is an excellent way to begin. I would recommend that you buy them from someone with similar values and beliefs as yourself, and that you thoroughly cleanse them before beginning to work with them. To cleanse them, if possible, (not if wood or other porous materials) leave them in sacred water for nine days and nights, or you could bury them in soil or earth for the same period of time.

Galdr

Galdr (or Galdor as it is known in Anglo-Saxon Heathenry) is the incantation and chanting of the Runes, as demonstrated earlier in this chapter. Galdr is a powerful tool in any magical situation magnifying the power of any Runes used with magical intent. Galdr is an excellent way to create sacred space and chanting the Runes is a formidable way of shifting the mood and atmosphere into a deeper more resonant plane. Indeed, simply chanting several particular Runes can be exchanged for most ritual workings. Examples of Galdr working can be found throughout the Eddas and poems, most notably in *Grógaldr* or Groa's Chant in the *Poetic Edda*. In the poem Svipdag who has been cursed by his stepmother, and forced to go on a dangerous journey, visits his dead mother's grave to ask for her help.

Chant me some chants – those which are good ones,
Mother, save your son!
(Grógaldr. 5. The Poetic Edda)

To which his mother, Groa chants or incants nine Galdr spells to aid him on his saga-journey.

Galdr can be utilised in Runic magic to enhance the potency of any Runic charms.

Bindrunes

Runes can be used in lots of different way within magic. Combining two or more Runes can be made into Bindrunes, which are magical sigils or talismans created for many different purposes, from house protection to health issues. A good example of a Bindrune is the most internationally recognised Bluetooth logo. When you are proficient in your understanding of each Rune's personality and nuances, you may be able to create your own Bindrunes. However, there are pitfalls, primarily that you might add incidental Runes to your Bindrune by mistake, and this Rune may have an altered or even negative effect on the overall outcome of the intention. If in doubt, ask a practiced creator to help you.

Anna is an artist who specialises in creating the most powerful Bindrunes in paintings and amulets. She very kindly gave me some insight into her creative process and her Heathen practice:

> *I am very solitary in my practice, which centres around honouring and working with the cycles of nature throughout the year, recognising these as literal and symbolic seasons and cycles in our lives also. I find it particularly interesting to learn how specific God's and figures from mythos connect with these seasons, elements, and natural spaces, such as specific animals, trees and weather phenomena, and just how significant these would have been to our ancestors and their understanding of all within the cosmos.*

She elaborated on her personal Runic practice:

> *Working with the runes is at the heart of all I do, and they constantly teach me new levels of understanding of our lived and emotional experiences – into the deeper meaning we so often seek. I see the importance of storytelling and exploring how we can relate to life through myth, and myth through life, not only from our ancestor's point of view, but by bringing that wisdom into the present to keep tradition alive and share that it is still very much relevant today.*

What drew you to creating bindrunes?

> *I felt very called to work with them more intensely, so started reading different books and gradually I began to notice the*

shape of runes in natural spaces and as I walked through Woodland. The more I studied them the more I realised the runes I would see often had a message for whatever was going on in my life or mind at the time, and they became a deeper part of my own spiritual practice. Through these processes I developed my connection with the runes, and that taught me that they can be used both to help navigate and understand challenging life experiences as well as beneficial or positive qualities we would like to possess in equal measure. I cast the runes in a specific way, and will read the messages they share with me, often using them for guidance or insight and exploring different perspectives.

What does a bindrune represent to you?

To me, a bindrune builds upon the wisdom and intention of each individual rune to create a collective meaning. Whilst they are a fairly modern construction and usage of the runes in this sense, they honour their history and allow us to incorporate ancient wisdom into our lives in the present day. Each bindrune I create has a very specific written message and intention, which is a vital part of its creation process. They each combine individual runes in a defined yet unique sequence, which creates layers of intentional interaction, working with the traditional interpretations and meanings we can infer from the rune poems as well as other trusted sources. There is a lot of space for personal interpretation and energetic inflection, which makes it a personal experience to me also.

Lastly, I asked Anna for any advice she would like to offer a new Heathen:

Listen to what calls to you and do your own research into different practices and ways of approaching Heathenism beyond popular culture as it can be very different. There are many incredible voices sharing wisdom and opinions, but not all of them may feel right to you, and it's ok to explore different paths and traditions, and find what feels best for you at a personal level.

Runic Magic

The Sagas and Eddas contain many examples of Runic inscriptions that were used magically, and holding powerful, even life changing significance. Apparently, random Runic letters, could predict the future, protect against misfortune, imbue and objects with different characteristics. Written down, they could be used as conjurations, curses, and spells.

In the *Volsunga Saga* poem, Lay of Sigrdrifa (the *Poetic Edda*), the former Valkyrie, Sigrdrifa or Brynhild offers the hero Sigurd magical Runes to aid him in gaining glory on his quests and battles ahead. Although we are not told exactly what Runes were offered, they include Victory-Runes which have to be carved into his sword and then he must "...invoke Tyr twice." (Stanza 6) Which implies Rune used is ᛏ Tyr. Sea-Runes which must be cut into the prow of the ship, (Stanza10) suggest ᛚ Logr the sea Rune from the Younger Futhark.

Within *Egil's Saga*, the first of the Icelandic Sagas, the hero Egil is extraordinarily gifted in Runic magic. Firstly, he saves himself from a poisoned horn of mead by carving Runes on the horn in his own blood, while reciting the following verse:

I carve Runes on this horn,
Redden words with my blood,
I chose words for the trees
Of the wild beast's ear-roots... (*horns)*
(Egil's Saga. P 68)

When the invocation is said, the horn shatters on the floor. Later in the saga, Egil is collecting taxes for the king and stops at a farmstead to take breakfast, when he spots a mysteriously sick girl. Upon finding out that someone has carved magical Runes to heal her, but to no avail, he immediately searches her bed and finding the whalebone, he throws it into the fire speaking a verse:

No man should carve Runes
Unless he can read them well;
Many a man goes astray
Around those dark letters..."
(*Egil's Saga*. p.141)

He then carves new Runic sigils, and the young woman is recovered.

From these examples, found within the key texts of the *Poetic Edda* and Icelandic Sagas, we can see a strong historical lineage for using Runes for a magical outcome. In all of these cases the Runes were carved into objects (such as on the prow of the ship, or whalebone above) making the object they were carved into, magical. Using these texts as a guide, objects could be carved with certain Runes to achieve a specific outcome. For example, ᚦ ᛇ ᛉ (Þorn, Eoh and Ilx) could be carved into a candle and burnt in a simple spell of protection. The Runes in this combination, represent (Þorn) striking or fighting back, (Eoh) defence and (Ilx) protection, (if we accept that the Ilx Rune connotates the elk, a creature that is very protective of its young). They could be written on paper and burnt over a candle whilst reciting their names (Galdr) adding another layer of power, or even written, painted or carved into a talisman that can be carried around or worn.

A talisman is something that is carried or worn and brings a specific objective, such as good fortune to the carrier/wearer. You will find jewellery with Runic symbols in most new age shops, and it is a clear example of the over commercialism of Runes, and alternative practices in recent years. However, as stated earlier, consider the energies a mass-produced object will bring to you, before you purchase it. It is probably best to know the creator has similar beliefs as yourself and will have created the talisman in a sacred way. Better still, create your own.

Chapter 10

Heathenry in the 21st Century

On the Pagan Federation website, Heathenry is listed as one of the predominant pagan spiritualities, alongside Wicca and Druidry.

I feel I would be remiss, however, if I didn't touch upon the difficult question that, if you aren't aware of, you should be. As with any aspect of modern life, Heathenry has its fair share of issues; and is sadly and erroneously linked to far-right extremism, Nazi ideals and racism.

Anyone who has studied the history of WW2 will be aware that the Nazis appropriated iconography and symbols from Norse mythology to symbolise their depraved and sick agenda especially in relation to racial purity. Their propaganda often utilised the work of Richard Wagner and his ring cycle opera, Der Ring Des Nibelungen, for example, meaning that the Operas, and Wagner's work is hardly preformed or played because of its associations with Nazism. Even today the news is saturated with senseless acts of violence against others; including mass shootings by individuals who claim affiliation with the Norse gods and Valhalla. On social media, it is sometimes hard to navigate through fake Heathen or Asatru posts, which far right groups often hijack to attempt to gain support for their pathetic ideas, making it a mine field for genuine and new Heathens to navigate. These vile and insidious associations are the complete and absolute opposite to what Heathenry is and what it stands for.

The Vikings were firstly explorers, they wanted to go to and settle in other lands and mixed successfully with other cultures, including through marriage. There is nothing in any of the mythology that supports racist agendas, or white supremacy and indeed many of the organisations I recommend in the Homework Chapter are far reaching with members all over the world. The best advice I can offer is to start with these recommended organisations, talk to members, make friends, and importantly when dealing with social media, if it doesn't seem or feel right, then steer clear of it.

If in any doubt whatsoever, please read Andrew Pardy's *The Kindred's Guide to Extremism* which is available as a downloadable PDF from Asatru UK and features detailed information about all extremist groups in the UK and beyond. You can also seek out one of the organisations below:

Asatru UK (www.asatru.org) The foremost inclusive Heathen Community in the UK.

Heathens Against Hate (www.heathensagainst.org)
An organisation who aims to bring Heathen communities together to educate each other, and non-Heathens on the difference between commonly held beliefs and practices and extremism.

The Troth (www.thetroth.org) One of the oldest inclusive organisations.

Alliance for Inclusive Heathenry (www.facebook.com/inclusive.heathenry) A Facebook group that promotes Heathenry as a pre-Christian faith for all those who seek it.

Heathenry is a fulfilling and beautiful faith, with no prerequisite of ancestry, no judgements based on sex, how you look, or why you're here. Diversity is strength and respect for all is paramount.

(Thanks to Andrew Pardy, who reviewed this chapter, offered insightful advice, and who gave me permission to use his guide on extremism in this chapter.)

Conclusion

Make It Yours!

What began for me with *The Hobbit* and a bag of Runes, has become a spiritual way of being in the world. Admittedly my Heathen journey is probably completely different from anyone else's, but we all share the same gods! Within this book we have looked at Heathenry with the aid of the sagas, myths, Eddas and other key texts. We have studied elements of history that give Heathenry a strong base and a broad context to how we practice today. We have examined rituals, Heathen holidays, the Gods, the Vaettir, the ancestors and the Runes. Many solitary Heathens have generously stepped forward to talk to me about how they practice their Heathenry today, which illustrates how much of a unique, and diverse path Heathenry is.

So, what's left for you to do now? You've done all your homework, had a go at rituals, talked to the Gods, made friends with your house spirits, honoured your ancestors, and tried out the Runes? Next is up to you...make it YOUR OWN!

And welcome to Heathenry!

Epilogue

Homework!

Here you will find essential reading, some organisations, and places to visit in relation to your Heathen quest. These are for anyone who is new to Heathenry, or unsure of where to start. I have tried to offer a synopsis and a review of each of the primary texts so as to allow you to evaluate which ones are suitable for you.

Texts

Please note: These would usually be texts or manuscripts that were written around the time period in which the events would have taken place. However, because most of the stories and sagas were handed down orally, many were lost, or destroyed during political and religious changes. Therefore, these works were composed with a few centuries difference but are the best sources available to us.

The Poetic Edda (Otherwise known as the Elder Edda)

This is comprised of compilation of Old Norse poems about the gods, their deeds, their wisdom and mythology. There are many versions of the *Poetic Edda,* each one offers a slightly different translation. The exact date of the poems is always under debate, but it's likely that many of them are original, at least in a fragmentary form. My personal copy is the Penguin Books translation by Carolyne Larrington. In my opinion she is an eminent academic scholar, whose notes and introduction are extremely useful in understanding the texts. This version includes *both* versions of the Voluspa, which I know not all versions have. This is extremely useful, not only because of ease of comparison, but there is no need to buy a second copy to compare. Other translators include Lee M. Hollander and Terry Bellows. I have heard that Hollander's translation is the most popular with modern Heathens, and his version is very accessible. Bellows' translation has a good balance between scholarly and accessibility. Jackson Crawford's version is highly acclaimed.

Since became Heathen, I have been drawn again and again to the Voluspa, the first poem in the Edda series. This is otherwise known as the Seeress's Prophecy. Odin is interrogating a Volva (Seeress) to see into the future and give him information about Ragnarök. The Volva tells him the whole cycle of time in Norse history from creation until after Odin's death and the new beginning. Interestingly, there are two versions of the Voluspa, the first and most known is from the *Codex Regius* an old Icelandic work, handwritten on forty-five sheets of vellum from the twelfth century. This invaluable manuscript is the sole source of many of the poems from the *Poetic Edda*. The second version, the *Hauksbók* is slightly later, from fourteenth century Iceland, and was created by Haukr Erlendsson. Much of this manuscript has been lost and Haukr is known to have copied the Sagas and Eddas from now long-lost earlier works.

The Prose Edda

This infamous book was written in the 13th century by the Icelander Snorri Sturluson. Snorri was a devout Christian and although he was essentially preserving the texts, his Christianity is very obvious and therefore we must assume that, although essential reading, his work is subjective. The *Prose Edda* consists of four sections: Prologue, which is a highly Christianised account of the Norse gods, including the suggestion that the gods were warriors who escaped from the Trojan war from classical mythology. Gylfaginning, which is presented in a question-and-answer format, rather like Vafthrudnir's Sayings from the *Poetic Edda*, in which aspects of Norse mythology, and the passing of the Norse mythological cycle are disclosed. Skáldskaparmál, which is divided into two separate parts, firstly a conversation between the Aesir god, Bragi, and Aegir, the god of the sea. This section contains all the major prose stories, much of the modern Norse mythology books are based around these tales. The second part is a list of poetic references on how to refer to the gods and other beings. An old translation by Jean Young is very readable, however, it is long out of print and fetches a high price second hand. Anthony Faulkes translation is more academic and accurate. My own copy is the Penguin Classics translation by Jesse Byock and is a scholarly version with good introduction and balanced notes about the texts. There are other versions and translations available.

Beowulf

You may be wondering why a poem set in Scandinavia with Swedish and Danish characters ended up firstly being an old English poem and how it is connected to the Anglo-Saxons. There is a supposition that the poem might be connected with the Sutton Hoo kings because they had close connections with Scandinavia and the royal dynasty from that area was the Wuffingas, who are likely related to the Geatish Wuffings.

There are numerous editions of *Beowulf* in modern English and many re-imaginings, including the excellent translation by Maria Dahvana Headley, which reinterprets the poem from a feminist perspective. Tolkien's edition is very extensive and because he was a professor of Anglo-Saxon literature, offers a strong academic commentary. Famous children's author, Michael Morpurgo, has adapted the story for a younger audience, meaning that it is accessible to the whole family; this version is a contemporary re-telling which, in turn, exposes future generations to a better understanding of history. My personal favourite is Seamus Heaney's narrative because it utilises the author's unique and beautiful poetic style to bring a breath of fresh air to the tale. *Beowulf* is most translated epic poem from Old English, and arguably the most important. Written anonymously around the tenth century, it was probably originally a much older tale, told orally and then latterly written down. If the poem was written down in pagan times, then the Christian themes were added later, and my feeling is that is so, because personally I find the areas written from a Christian perspective don't flow as well. However, there is much documented evidence from graves of both Christian and Pagan practices, so it is entirely possible that both religions were practiced simultaneously. The original manuscript is known as the *Nowell Codex,* which is housed in the British Library

The now famous story tells of how Beowulf, a heroic Geat from southern Sweden, helps the king of the Danes, Hrothgar, who has been under attack in his mead house for the past twelve years by a monster named Grendel. When Beowulf manages to slay the monster, Grendel's mother takes her revenge but is unsuccessful. After this, Beowulf becomes king of the Geats and some fifty years later he is mortally wounded killing a dragon. A barrow is erected in his memory.

The Sagas

The Sagas are essentially stories and histories written in a prose style. They cover many aspects of the Viking era, such as settlements in Iceland and Greenland, and the stories of kings and heroes. It's hard to believe but there are over one hundred sagas. *The Sagas of the Icelanders,* which was written in the 12th and 13th centuries CE, is one of the most famous, primarily focuses on the genealogy and family history of the first settlers. In a nutshell, the *Saga of the Icelanders* is a book about the beginning of Iceland in pre-Christian times. Contained within Icelandic Sagas are: *The Laxdæla Saga,* which is a series tragic stories concentrated on generations of one warrior family who were all descended from Ketill Flatnose. *The Gisla Saga* which follows the story of the outlaw and poet Gisli Sursson, who stayed on the run for thirteen years after killing one of his brothers-in-law. Meanwhile the *Njáls Saga* describes events during the Icelandic Commonwealth, from 960 – 1020 CE. This time period was known for its turbulence and civil wars. The *Sagas of the Icelanders* is a significant tome and can be at times a little stuffy. However, several of the sagas are available individually, such as the *Saga of Erik The Red* and the *Vinland Sagas,* which are a history of the occupation of Greenland and the discovery of America. I would recommend persevering with them because they not only offer a firsthand history of this time period but illuminate the peoples' pre-Christian beliefs and customs.

Legendary Sagas were set in a time period before Iceland was settled, and include the famous *Völsunga Saga,* which is featured in some versions of the *Poetic Edda.* It is the story of one of the most renowned heroes of Norse mythology, Sigurd who kills the dragon Fafnir and then falls tragically in love with a Valkyrie, Brynhild. Latterly the *Völsunga Saga* was re-imagined in Wagner's famous Ring Cycle Operas and was said to be an inspiration for J. R.R. Tolkien's *Lord of the Rings.*

Modern Versions of the Myths

The popularity of the Norse myths only seems to increase, largely thanks to computer video games, TV programmes and films featuring the heroes and gods of the Vikings. If you search on the internet for books of Norse myths, you will be met with a whole plethora of them, many of which are excellent introductions to the stories of the heroes and gods of Norse mythology.

Folklore

Exploring, firstly, the folklore and stories from the area in which you live, gives you an enriched and deepening connection to your home. It will undoubtably clarify how the local landscape was understood in the past. With this framework you can build relationships with your place, and the spirits who live there. Most folklore stories are at least entertaining, and with careful study, can reveal many aspects of nature that perhaps you had not considered.

I would also recommend studying the folklore and tales from Scandinavia, because in a similar way to examining your own folklore, this explains how earlier generations perceived their world and how this was fed into Heathen understanding. Recently two books on Danish and Icelandic folklore have been published by the History Press and are good starting points; *Icelandic Folk Tales by* Hjörleifur Helgi Stefánsson and *Danish Folk Tales by* Svend-Erik Engh. There are also many older books on Norwegian and Swedish Folklore, so it's worth checking online marketplaces and thrift stories.

Organisations

There are many organisations and Heathen groups in the world, here, I am only offering a guide to the ones I have any first-hand experience of. These are all recognised bodies in Heathenry are inclusive in their ethos. Please scrutinise their codes of practice and research them fully to make sure you are happy with them before you make any form of contact.

A word of warning here: There are many so-called groups on the internet that on the outside appear to be innocent and claim to be Heathen. Do Take care! Sadly, there are some who are politically far-right, extremist, and/or white supremacists. **If in doubt, don't!**

UK

Asatru UK: Formed in 2013, this is the main Heathen UK community. They have an online website and community group on Facebook, as well as local groups all over the country. Every year they have a gathering in the summer and winter, which

includes rituals, music and comradery. Asatru UK is open to anyone who is interested in Heathenry in the UK. Their website has some excellent resources for people who are starting out on the Heathen path, and they produce several of their own booklets including guides to key texts and rituals.
https://www.asatruuk.org/

The Pagan Federation: Although not specifically a Heathen organisation, the Pagan federation is an umbrella for all pagan faiths. Established in 1971, its aim is to promote paganism and protect pagans against discrimination. The PF offers advice on advocacy and education and works with other faith groups to create an equal society.
https://www.paganfed.org/

USA

The Troth: Originally established in 1987, The Troth is a religious organisation in the USA, although anyone from anywhere can join. They run programmes and educational projects and courses that promote all forms of the Northern Traditions. They actively work to promote inclusivity and work against separatist ideas.
https://thetroth.org/

Online Organisations

Heathen Women United – UK, Ireland and Iceland: This is a growing online community aimed specifically at women Heathens. They have an informal online Zoom meeting once a month.
https://www.facebook.com/groups/476659712855236

There are many more organisations that you can look into, and it's easy enough to search online, but please bear in mind my warning above. The above organisations are an excellent starting point, are inclusive and have connections with other inclusive Heathen communities.

Places

There are many places that are important to Heathens, globally. In my own personal Heathen practice, walking and immersing in the landscape, is a devotional practice. The Gods and Vaettir, (spirits of place, see Chapter 6) are everywhere, and for example, when working with the Vaettir, you just need to attune yourself to the land, breathe deeply, listen deeply and speak to them.

You may remember I mentioned Grimes Graves in the introduction – the place I first encountered Odin, and certainly some places are historically significant – holding that ancestral connection to the Vikings or Anglo-Saxons. Other places may be less obvious, such as mountains or the shoreline, liminal spaces that are portals, or focal points for the sacred. It could be that you find a place that is important personally to you, one that is not mentioned in any 'how to' guide but is nonetheless one in which you find the meaning you need.

The few places listed below are in no way extensive or exclusive and the idea is that they, as examples, will encourage you to research and find more.

Denmark

Lindholm Høje: Situated near Aalborg, Lindholm Høje is a major Viking burial site and settlement featuring over seven hundred stone ship burials dating from the Iron Age until the end of the Viking Age.

Iceland

The Iceland of today was founded by Viking settlers around the middle of the nine centuries, prior to this, Iceland was unpopulated. The country is truly a land of fire and ice, with volcanoes and vast frozen wastelands in winter. The Icelandic language is the closest living language to Old Norse.

Norway

The Midgard Vikingsenter: Situated in Borre southern Norway, the Viking Centre has several monumental burial mounds which you can visit. The mounds date from 600-950 CE and at the time the land was agricultural, meaning they would be clearly visible to anyone sailing through the Oslo Fjord.

Sweden

Gamla Uppsala: An hour away from Stockholm, Gamla Uppsala was probably the most significant ritual site in the Viking Age. Today there are three remaining burial mounds, and many smaller satellite mounds.

Birka: The island of Birka is in the Stockholm peninsula, and accessible by boat. It is widely considered to be Sweden's first city, and the central hub for trading for over two hundred years. Birka has over four thousand graves.

UK

Unst, Shetland: The island of Unst is the northern most part of the United Kingdom and only two hundred miles west of Norway. It is said to be the first place the Vikings set foot on in the North Atlantic. Archaeologically, Unst has the highest concentration of rural domestic remains in Europe. All of which can be seen in the landscape. At Haroldwick there is a replica longship based on the Gokstad ship.

Sutton Hoo: The site of two Anglo-Saxon cemeteries dating from the 6th-7th centuries CE. It is famous for its ship burial which was discovered in 1938. The site contained many treasures including the famous Sutton Hoo Helmet in the British Museum.

Bibliography

Andersson. Gunnar. *The Viking World* – A Publication by the Swedish History Museum. 2021.

Anglo-Saxon Chronicle. Translated by G.N. Garmonsway. J.M. Dent & Sons. 1953

Blain. Jenny. *Understanding Wyrd: The Norns & The Tree.* Wyrds Well. 2000.

Blain. Jenny. *Wights and Ancestors.* Wyrds Well. 2000.

Branston. Brian. *Lost Gods of England.* BCA. 1974.

Burgess. Melvin. *Loki.* Coronet. 2023.

Byatt. A. S. *Ragnarök.* Canongate Books. 2011.

Carver. Martin, Sanmark. Alex. Semple. Sarah. (eds) *Signals of Belief in Early England.* Oxbow Books. 2010.

Coultas. Dan (Ed.) *The Asatru UK Book of Blots.* Asatru UK Publications. 2021.

Dahvana Headley. Maria. *Beowulf.* Scribe Publications. 2020.

Daimler. Morgan *Freya: Meeting the Norse Goddess of Magic.* Moon Books. 2023.

Daimler. Morgan. *The Norse Pantheon.* Moon Books. 2022.

Daimler. Morgan. *Odin.* Moon Books. 2017.

Daimler. Morgan. *Thor.* Moon Books. 2019.

Eggers. Robert. (Dir) The Northman. 2022. Universal Pictures.

Ellis-Davidson. Hilda. *Gods and Myths of Northern Europe.* Penguin Books. 1964.

Ellis-Davidson. Hilda. *The Lost Beliefs of Northern Europe.* Routledge. 1993.

Ellis-Davidson. Hilda. *Scandinavian Mythology.* Littlehampton Books. 1969.

Elli-Davidson. Hilda and Gelling Peter. *The Chariot of the Sun.* J. M. Dent and Sons. 1969.

Gaiman. Neil. *American Gods.* Healine. 2005.

Gaiman. Neil. *Norse Mythology.* Bloomsbury. 2017.

Gerrard. Katie. *Odin's Gateway*. Avalonia. 2009.

Grimm, Jacob. *Teutonic Mythology. Vol. I.* W. Swan & Allen. 1882

Grundy. Stephen. essay "Freyja and Frigg" in *Concepts of the Goddess*. Ed. Sandra Billingham and Miranda Green. Routledge. 1996.

Heaney. Seamus. *Beowulf*. Faber and Faber. 1999.

Herbert. Kathleen. *Lost Gods of England*. Anglo-Saxon Books. 1994.

Holmes. Kylie. *Pagan Portals: Runes*. Moon Books. 2013.

Hutton. Ronald. *Pagan Britain*. Yale University Press. 2013.

Jarman. Cat. *River Kings*. Williams Collins. 2021.

Krasskova. Galina. Exploring the Northern Tradition. New Page Books. 2005.

Lafayllve. Patricia. M. *A Practical Heathen's Guide to Asatru*. Llewellyn Publications. 2013.

Larrington. Carolyne. *The Poetic Edda*. Oxford World Classics. 2014.

Lecouteux. Claude. *Demons and Spirits of the Land*. Inner Traditions. 2015.

Lecouteux. Claude. *The Tradition of Household Spirits*. Inner Traditions. 2013.

Lindow. John. *Norse Mythology*. Oxford University Press. 2001.

Loptson. Dagulf. *Loki: Trickster and Transformer*. Moon Books. 2020.

McClain. Ryan. *Frigg – Beloved Queen of Asgard*. Moon Books. 2024.

Morris. Marc. The Anglo-Saxons. Penguin Books. 2021.

Moon. Irisanya. *The Norns, Weavers of Fate and Magick*. Moon Books. 2023.

Orchard. Andy. *Dictionary of Norse Myth and Legend*. Cassell. 1997.

Owen. Gale. *Rites and Religions of the Anglo-Saxons*. Barns and Noble.1981.

Pardy. Andrew. *The Kindred's Guide to Pagan Extremism.* (PDF) Sleipnir Consulting. 2024.

Parker. Charles. *The Ancient Crosses of Gosforth and Cumberland.* Eliot Stock. 1896.

Parker Eleanor, *Winters In the World.* Reaktion Books.2022

Patterson. Rachel. *Gods and Goddesses of England.* Moon Books. 2023.

Pollington. Stephen. *Rudiments of Runelore. Anglo-Saxon Books.* 1995.

Price. Neil. *The Children of Ash & Elm.* Penguin Books. 2020.

Ramirez. Janina. *Femina.* Penguin Books. 2022.

Richards. Julian. *Blood of the Vikings.* B.B.C. Books. 2001.

Roberts. Alice. *Buried.* Simon & Schuster. 2022.

Roberts. Alice. *Crypt.* Simon & Schuster. 2024.

Shakespeare. William. *Macbeth.* Wordsworth Editions. 1992.

Simek. Rudolf. *A Dictionary of Norse Mythology.* D.S. Brewer. 2007.

Smiley. Jane (Ed.) *The Sagas of the Icelanders.* Penguin Classics. 1997.

Stratford. Brice. *Anglo-Saxon Myths.* Batsford. 2022.

Stowell. Louie. *Loki – A Bad God's Guide to Being Good.* Walker Books. 2022.

Sturluson. Snorri. *The Prose Edda.* Translated by Jesse. L. Byock. Penguin Classics. 2005.

Swaffington. S. A. *The Supernatural World of the Anglo-Saxons.* Independently Published. 2017.

Swanton. Michael. The Anglo-Saxon Chronicle. Routledge. 1998.

Tacitus. *Germanica.* Translated by A. R. Birley. Oxford World Classics. 2009.

Wallis, Faith. *Bede: The Reckoning of Time.* Liverpool University Press.1999

Winroth. Anders *The Conversion of Scandinavia: Vikings, Merchants, and Missionaries in the Remaking of Northern Europe.* Yale University Press. 2012.

Williams. Thomas. *Viking Britian*. Williams Collins. 2017.
Wood. Michael. *In Search of the Dark Ages*. (A History of Anglo-Saxon England.) Penguin Books. 1981.

MOON BOOKS

PAGANISM & SHAMANISM

What is Paganism? A religion, a spirituality, an alternative belief system, nature worship? You can find support for all these definitions (and many more) in dictionaries, encyclopaedias, and text books of religion, but subscribe to any one and the truth will evade you. Above all Paganism is a creative pursuit, an encounter with reality, an exploration of meaning and an expression of the soul. Druids, Heathens, Wiccans and others, all contribute their insights and literary riches to the Pagan tradition. Moon Books invites you to begin or to deepen your own encounter, right here, right now.

If you have enjoyed this book, why not tell other readers by posting a review on your preferred book site.

Bestsellers from Moon Books

Keeping Her Keys
An Introduction to Hekate's Modern Witchcraft
Cyndi Brannen
Blending Hekate, witchcraft and personal development together to create
a powerful new magickal perspective.
Paperback: 978-1-78904-075-3 ebook 978-1-78904-076-0

Journey to the Dark Goddess
How to Return to Your Soul
Jane Meredith
Discover the powerful secrets of the Dark Goddess and transform your depression, grief and pain into healing and integration.
Paperback: 978-1-84694-677-6 ebook: 978-1-78099-223-5

Shamanic Reiki
Expanded Ways of Working with Universal Life Force Energy
Llyn Roberts, Robert Levy
Shamanism and Reiki are each powerful ways of healing; together, their power multiplies. Shamanic Reiki introduces techniques to help healers and Reiki practitioners tap ancient healing wisdom.
Paperback: 978-1-84694-037-8 ebook: 978-1-84694-650-9

Southern Cunning
Folkloric Witchcraft in the American South
Aaron Oberon
Modern witchcraft with a Southern flair, this book is a journey through the folklore of the American South and a look at the power these stories hold for modern witches.
Paperback: 978-1-78904-196-5 ebook: 978-1-78904-197-2

Bestsellers from Moon Books
Pagan Portals Series

The Morrigan

Meeting the Great Queens

Morgan Daimler

Ancient and enigmatic, the Morrigan reaches out to us. On shadowed wings and in raven's call, meet the ancient Irish goddess of war, battle, prophecy, death, sovereignty, and magic.

Paperback: 978-1-78279-833-0 ebook: 978-1-78279-834-7

The Awen Alone

Walking the Path of the Solitary Druid

Joanna van der Hoeven

An introductory guide for the solitary Druid, The Awen Alone will accompany you as you explore, and seek out your own place within the natural world.

Paperback: 978-1-78279-547-6 ebook: 978-1-78279-546-9

Moon Magic

Rachel Patterson

An introduction to working with the phases of the Moon, what they are and how to live in harmony with the lunar year and to utilise all the magical powers it provides.

Paperback: 978-1-78279-281-9 ebook: 978-1-78279-282-6

Hekate

A Devotional

Vivienne Moss

Hekate, Queen of Witches and the Shadow-Lands, haunts the pages of this devotional bringing magic and enchantment into your lives.

Paperback: 978-1-78535-161-7 ebook: 978-1-78535-162-4